THΓ
THE

MW01535208

BY

E. M. WILMOT-BUXTON

F.R.Hist.S.

AUTHOR OF
'BRITAIN LONG AGO' 'THE BOOK OF RUSTEM'
'TOLD BY THE NORTHMEN' ETC.

GEORGE G. HARRAP & CO. LTD.
LONDON BOMBAY SYDNEY

First published December 1910

The First Crusaders in Sight of Jerusalem

Contents

I. The Story of Mohammed the Prophet
II. Mohammed as Conqueror
III. The Spread of Islam
IV. The Rise of Chivalry
V. The Story of Peter the Hermit
VI. The Story of the Emperor Alexios and the First Crusade
VII. The Siege of Antioch
VIII. The Holy City is won
IX. Bernard of Clairvaux and the Second Crusade
X. The Loss of Jerusalem
XI. The Story of the Third Crusade
XII. The Adventures of Richard Lion-Heart
XIII. The Story of Dandolo, the Blind Doge
XIV. The Forsaking of the High Enterprise
XV. The Story of the Latin Empire of Constantinople
XVI. The Story of the Children's Crusade
XVII. The Emperor Frederick and the Sixth Crusade
XVIII. The Story of the Seventh Crusade
XIX. The Crusade of St Louis
XX. The Story of the Fall of Acre
XXI. The Story of the Fall of Constantinople
XXII. The Effect of the Crusades

List of Books Consulted

Illustrations

The First Crusaders in Sight of Jerusalem . . .
Frontispiece
The Vision of Mohammed
Pilgrims of the Eleventh Century journeying to the Holy
City
The Preaching of Peter the Hermit
Duke Godfrey marching through Hungary
Robert of Normandy at Dorylæum
The Storming of Jerusalem
King Louis surrounded by the Turks
Richard and Philip at the Siege of Acre
Richard of England utterly defeats the Army of Saladin
The Fleet of the Fifth Crusade sets Sail from Venice
The Children crossing the Alps
John of Brienne attacking the River Tower
The Landing of St Louis in Egypt
The Last Fight of William Longsword
The Fall of Acre
Map of the Crusades

The Story of the Crusades

CHAPTER I

The Story of Mohammed the Prophet

A poor shepherd people roaming unnoticed in the deserts of Arabia: a Hero-Prophet sent down to them with a word they could believe: See! the unnoticed becomes world-notable, the small has grown world-great.

CARLYLE: *Hero as Prophet.*

The two hundred years which cover, roughly speaking, the actual period of the Holy War, are crammed with an interest that never grows dim. Gallant figures, noble knights, generous foes, valiant women, eager children, follow one another through these centuries, and form a pageant the colour and romance of which can never fade, for the circumstances were in themselves unique. The two great religious forces of the world—Christianity and Islam, the Cross and the Crescent—were at grips with one another, and for the first time the stately East, with its suggestion of mystery, was face to face with the brilliant West, wherein the civilisation and organisation of Rome were at last prevailing over the chaos of the Dark Ages.

A very special kind of interest, moreover, belongs to the story of the Crusades in that the motive of the wars was the desire to rescue from the hands of unbelievers

> *Those holy fields*
> *Over whose acres walked those blessed feet*
> *Which, fourteen hundred year before, were nailed*
> *For our advantage on the bitter cross.*

But we shall see, as we read the story, that this was only a part of the real motive power which inspired and sustained the Holy War.

Even if the land of Palestine and the Holy City, Jerusalem, had never fallen into the hands of the Saracens, some such war was inevitable. The East was knocking at the doors of the West with no uncertain sound. An extraordinary force had come into existence during the four centuries that immediately preceded the First Crusade, which threatened to dominate the whole of the Western world. It was a religious force—always stronger and more effective than any other; and it was only repelled with the greatest difficulty by Christendom, inspired, not so much by the motive of religion, as by that curious mixture of romance and adventurous design which we call chivalry.

Let us try, then, first of all, to get some idea of these Men of the East, the Mohammedans or Saracens, who managed to keep Europe in a state of constant turmoil for upwards of five centuries, and to do that we must go back to the latter years of the sixth century after Christ.

About fifty miles from the shores of the Red Sea stands the city of Mecca, one of the few important towns to be found on the fringe of the great sandy desert of Arabia. During hundreds of years Mecca had been the venerated bourne of pilgrims, for, embedded in the walls of the sacred building known as the Kaaba, was the "pure white stone," said to have fallen from heaven on the day that Adam and Eve took their sorrowful way from the gates of Paradise.

The Arabs, or Saracens, of these early days were closely connected with their neighbours, the Jews of Palestine, and claimed the same descent from Abraham through Ishmael, the outcast son. They believed in the existence of God, whom, to some extent, they worshipped, under the name of Allah. But they were deeply interested in nature-worship: the sun, moon, and stars were their deities. They bowed down before the "pure white stone" in the Kaaba, now from its frequent handling rather black than white. They peopled the whole realm of nature—oceans, rivers, mountains, caves—with spirits good and evil, called "jinns" or genii, made, not of clay, like mortal men, but of pure flame of fire.

Once upon a time these jinns were said to have lived in heaven, and to have worshipped the Lord of Hosts; but having rebelled, under the leadership of Iblis, against Allah, they were cast forth, and descended to the earth, where they became sometimes a pest and annoyance to men, and sometimes their servants.

Many legends concerning these spirits are to be found in the Koran, the sacred book of the Mohammedans. One of these tells how the jinns were wont to roam round about the gates of heaven, peeping and listening and catching here and there a little of the converse of the angels. But these were only isolated words, or disjointed phrases; and the mischievous jinns, hoping that evil would come of these odds and ends of conversation separated from their context, whispered them industriously in the ears of the sons of men. These the latter, always eager to know more of the Unseen World, readily accepted, and invariably put a wrong interpretation upon them. Hence arose superstition, black magic, false prophecies, evil omens, and all such things as had in them the germ of truth, but had been misunderstood and misapplied.

From the midst of this imaginative and nature-worshipping people there arose the prophet who was to found one of the most powerful religious sects in the world.

In the year 570 A.D., in the city of Mecca, a boy child came to the young mother Amina, to comfort her in her widowhood for the husband who had died a few weeks before. Tradition has been active regarding the cradle of this child, the young Mohammed. He is said to have exclaimed at the moment of birth, "Allah is great! There is no God but Allah, and I am His prophet."

That same day an earthquake was reported to have overturned the gorgeous palace of Persia; a wild camel was seen in a vision to be overthrown by a slender Arab horse; and Iblis, the evil spirit, leader of the malignant jinns, was cast into the depths of ocean.

What is actually known about the matter is that the babe was presented to his tribe on the seventh day after his birth, and was named Mohammed, the "Praised One," in prophetic allusion to his future fame.

For the first five years of his life, according to Arabian custom, the child was sent to a foster-mother in the mountains that he might grow up sturdy and healthy. Soon after the end of that period, his mother died, and he was left to the care of his uncle, Abu Talib, a wealthy trader, who was so fond and proud of his nephew that he let the boy accompany him on many of his long caravan journeys to Yemen or Syria. Thus the young Mohammed became intimately acquainted with all sorts and conditions of men. He had no books, but he was an eager listener to the poems recited by the bards in the market-place of each great town. He quickly absorbed the legends and superstitions of his country, formed his own opinion about the idol-worship practised by many of the Arab tribes, and was present on a great historic occasion, when an oath was taken by his tribe in alliance with others, to be the champions of the weak and the avengers of the oppressed. Moreover, since his own home was at Mecca, the "Fair of all Arabia," the centre of trade for India, Syria, Egypt, and Italy, the boy had plenty of chances of acquiring that knowledge of the world which subsequently served him in good stead as a leader of men.

He grew up a silent, thoughtful youth, loved and respected by his companions, who named him El Amin, the "Faithful One." He was notable too for his good looks, for his bright dark eyes, clear brown skin, and for a curious black vein that swelled between his eyebrows when he was moved to anger. He had wide opportunities for thought and meditation, since, as was the case with most Arabs, his occupation was for years that of a shepherd on the hillsides of his native city. Eventually, at his uncle's wish, he became camel-driver and conductor of the caravan of a certain rich widow named Kadija. The long journey to Syria was undertaken with success, and on his return the widow Kadija looked upon the young man of twenty-five with eyes of favour. She imagined she saw two angels shielding him with their wings from the scorching sunshine, and, taking this for an indication that he was under the special protection of Allah, sent her sister to him, according to a common custom of Arabia, to intimate her willingness to be his bride.

So the poor camel-driver became the husband of the wealthy Kadija, and a very happy marriage it turned out to be. Six children came to gladden the peaceful home, of whom the youngest, Fatima, was to play a part in future history. To all appearances these were years of calm existence, almost of stagnation, for Mohammed; but all the time the inner life of the man was growing, expanding, throwing out fresh tentacles of thought and inquiry, as he brooded upon the condition, and especially upon the religious condition, of his fellow-countrymen. For the Arabs of his day were a degenerate race, much given to drinking and gaming and evil passions. They thought nothing of burying their girl-children alive after birth, as unworthy to be brought up. They had no heroic ideals, and their religion was becoming more and more vague and shadowy where it was not given over entirely to the worship of idols.

It was the Arab custom to keep the month Ramadan as a kind of Lent, in fasting, in seclusion and meditation; and Mohammed, during that period, was wont to retire to a cave in a mountain near Mecca, sometimes with Kadija, sometimes quite alone. There he was overtaken on one occasion by strange trances and visions in which uttered weird prophetic sentences. He subsequently confided to Kadija, who was with him at that time, that he had made the Great Discovery; that all these idols, and sacred stones, and empty phrases of religion were nothing—nothing at all. "That God is great, and that there is nothing else great. He is Reality. Wooden idols are not real; but He is real—He made us and protects us; hence *We must submit to Allah, and strive after righteousness.*" This was to be the keynote of the faith to be known as *Islam*.

After this revelation had come to him, Mohammed continued his life of thought and meditation for some time, until he was nearly forty years of age. He may have spoken of his conviction to his friends, but he does not seem to have gained much sympathy, and rather he appears to have earned the reputation of a dreamer. But about the year 610, as he was wandering over the wild hillsides, the clear call came, as it is bound to come to the humble, listening soul. He had lain down to sleep when, in a vision, he heard three times his name repeated, and the third time saw the angel Gabriel—in whose existence both Arabs and Jews believed—who spoke to him and bade him

Cry! in the name of Allah!
In the name of Allah,
Who hath created man.

At first Mohammed was much disturbed by this message, which he did not clearly understand. He feared he was under the influence of magic, and was filled with dread of falling into the hands of jinns. After a visit to his home, he again sought the mountain, intending in his harassed state of mind to put an end to his life. Each time he attempted this, something restrained him, and as he sat at length in despair upon the ground wrapped in his cloak, the angel once more appeared, saying—

O thou that art covered,
   Arise and preach,
And magnify Allah!
   Purify thy garments,

Shun all evils,
Grant not money on usury,
Wait patiently for Allah.
When the trump shall blow shall be distress for unbelievers.

From that time the vocation of Mohammed was clear. He was to go forth and preach to a nation of idolaters that there was one God, and only one, who might claim their worship. Never again did he hesitate, nor, on the other hand, did he begin his work in haste. He still sojourned among the mountains, where he was visited by his uncle, Abu Talib, and by the little son of the latter, a boy called Ali.

"What calls you here, Mohammed?" asked the puzzled Abu, "and what religion do you now profess?"

Said Mohammed: "I profess the religion of Allah, of His angels and His prophets, the religion of Abraham. Allah has commissioned me to preach this to men, and to urge them to embrace it. Nought would be more worthy of thee, O my uncle, than to adopt the true faith, and to help me to spread it."

But Abu Talib replied: "Son of my brother, I can never forsake the faith of my fathers; but if thou art attacked, I will defend thee." Then to his young son Ali he continued: "Hesitate not to follow any advice he giveth thee, for Mohammed will never lead thee into any wrong way."

The first attempts of Mohammed to begin his work of conversion met with small success. We have good authority for the proverb that "a prophet has no honour in his own country," and in Mohammed's case his task was made supremely difficult by the fact that Mecca would no longer be the goal of thousands of pilgrims every year if the Arabs were to give up the worship of the idols of the Kaaba, which numbered, exclusive of the "pure white stone" itself, some three hundred and sixty-five images. Now the whole prosperity of the city depended upon the caravan trade brought by these pilgrims, as well as on the profits made out of providing food and shelter for such vast numbers. Realising this, Mohammed made no attempt at a public proclamation of the new faith for the first three years, but contented himself with training two or three converts to be his helpers in the future.

His faithful wife Kadija was with him heart and soul, and to her, first of all, he disclosed the details which the angel had revealed to him in a vision, as to the particular acts of ritual, forms of prayer, and actual doctrine which *Islam*, as their faith was called, demanded of its followers. The essential fact of this religion was a belief in Allah as the one true God, in a future life of happiness or misery after death, and in Mohammed himself as the Prophet of Allah, whom they were bound to obey. It was essentially a practical faith, however, and, in addition to prayer five times a day, the Islamite or *Moslem* must give alms to the poor, be perfectly honest in weighing and measuring, be absolutely truthful, and keep strictly to all agreements made. Many minor details were afterwards added to these, and the whole were gradually written down in the *Koran*, the sacred book of Islam. This, of course, was not done till many years later, when Mohammed had drawn up a moral and social code which he hoped would reform the whole world. In the meantime he had a hard struggle before him.

One of his first followers was the child Ali, who, though but eleven years old, became his constant companion in his lonely rambles, and eagerly received his instructions. A freed slave, and Abu Bekr, a man of official rank, enthusiastic for the new faith, were his next converts. In vain did Mohammed call together the members of his tribe, saying unto them—

"Never has an Arab offered to his people such precious things as I now present to you—happiness in this life, and joys for ever in the next. Allah has bidden me call men to Him—Who will join me in the sacred work and become my brother?"

Deep silence followed this appeal, broken only by the high, childish voice of little Ali, who cried out—

"I, Prophet of Allah, I will join you!"

Quite seriously Mohammed received the offer, saying to the assembled throng, "Behold my brother, my *Kalif*! Listen to him. Obey his commands."

Soon after this appeal to his own tribe, a spirit of active opposition arose among the men of Mecca, so much so that the chief men came to Abu Talib and warned him that if he did not prevail upon Mohammed to hold his peace and give up these new doctrines, they would take up arms against him and his supporters. Much alarmed at this protest, Abu Talib implored his nephew to keep his new-formed faith to himself. But Mohammed answered, "O my uncle, even if the sun should descend on my right hand and the moon on my left to fight against me, ordering me to hold my peace or perish, I would not waver from my purpose."

Then, thinking that the friend he loved so well was about to desert him, he turned away and wept. But the old Abu, touched to the heart, cried out, "Come back, O my nephew! Preach whatever doctrine thou wilt. I swear to thee that not for a moment will I desert thy side."

Opposition soon took the form of misrepresentation. The enemies of Mohammed would lie in wait for the pilgrims going up to the Kaaba and warn them to beware of a dangerous magician, whose charms sowed discord in the household, dividing husband and wife, parent and child. But this had the natural effect of making strangers much more curious about Mohammed than they would otherwise have been. They made their own inquiries, and though few converts were the result, the reputation of the Prophet, in a more or less misleading form, was gradually spread by them throughout the length and breadth of Arabia.

Meantime, Mohammed himself was the object of open insult in the streets of Mecca, as well as of actual violence. One effect of this, however, was to bring over to his side another uncle, Hamza by name who had been one of his fiercest opponents. Hearing of some new outrage, he hastened to the Kaaba and stood forth openly as the champion of the Prophet.

"*I* am of the new religion! Return *that*, if you dare!" he cried, dealing a vigorous blow at one of the angry and astonished assembly. They drew back in awe, and Hamza, the "Lion of Allah," became one of the most ardent followers of Islam.

The tide of persecution, however, was not stayed, and at length Mohammed, unable to protect his followers from the violence he was willing to endure himself, persuaded them to take refuge in Abyssinia, under the protection of the Christian king.

Furious at this, the men of Mecca placed Mohammed and his whole family under a ban for three long years, during which the Faithful nearly perished of hunger, for no man might buy of them or sell to them or have any kind of intercourse with them. This ban was removed at the end of three years, but then a worse blow fell upon the Prophet. Kadija, his faithful, loving wife, and Abu Talib, his friend and protector, both died. The death of Abu led to a renewal of persecution; very few fresh converts were made; failure met him on every side. The only ray of light in this period of gloom was the discovery that twelve pilgrims journeying from the distant city of Medina had already become followers of Islam from what they had heard of the new faith as taught by Mohammed. These men he gladly instructed more fully, and sent them back as missionaries to their own city.

In the midst of his depression and disheartened forebodings for the future, Mohammed was vouchsafed a marvellous vision or dream.

"Awake, thou that sleepest!" cried a voice like a silver trumpet, and there appeared to him an angel of wonderful brightness, who bade him mount the winged steed, *Borak*, the Lightning, and ascend to the Temple at Jerusalem. Thence by a ladder of light, Mohammed rose to the first heaven, made of pure silver, and lighted by stars suspended by chains of gold. There he was embraced as the chief of prophets by Adam, the first created man.

Thence he proceeded to the second heaven, which was of steel, and there he was greeted by Noah. The third heaven, where Joseph met him, was brilliant with precious stones. There too sat the Angel of Death, writing down the names of all who were to be born, and blotting out the names of those whose time had come to die. In the fourth heaven Aaron showed to him the Angel of Vengeance, in whose hands was a fiery spear. In the fifth Moses spoke with him and wept to see one who was going to lead to Paradise more of the Chosen People than he, their prophet. In the sixth, of marvellous brightness, Abraham occupied chief place; and Mohammed was even allowed to penetrate further to the seventh heaven, where Allah, His glory veiled, gave him instructions as to the doctrines of Islam, and bade him command his followers to utter fifty prayers a day.

When the Prophet returned to Moses, the latter pointed out that the number was too much to expect of Arabs, and bade him ask Allah to reduce it. In answer to his supplications, Allah said at first that forty prayers would be satisfactory, but Mohammed pleaded earnestly for further relief, and at last the number was fixed at five, at which it remains to this day. "Allahu akbar—Prayer is better than sleep! There is no God but Allah! He giveth life and He dieth not! O thou bountiful! Thy mercy ceaseth not! My sins are great, greater is Thy mercy! I praise His perfection! Allahu akbar!"

Still, five times a day, the peculiar cry of the "mullah" is heard from the tower of prayer, giving the signal for the follower of Islam to turn towards Mecca, throw himself on his face, and utter the prescribed words.

The Vision of Mohammed

The Vision of Mohammed

Much inspired by this wonderful dream, Mohammed was further encouraged by the news that seventy men of Medina had joined the ranks of Islam and were about to meet him on the hillside beyond Mecca, with intent to induce him, if possible, to take up his future abode in their city, leaving his birthplace to its fate. There, under the dark midnight sky, these men bound themselves to worship Allah only, to obey the Prophet, and to fight in defence of him and his followers.

"And what will be our reward?" asked one.

"Paradise!" replied Mohammed briefly.

And then the oath was sworn; while the Prophet, on his side, promised to live and die with his new converts when the time was ripe.

The meeting had, however, been watched by spies, who reported all to the men of Mecca; and a new persecution arose, so bitter that most of the "Faithful," as the followers of Mohammed came to be called, fled at once to Medina. Mohammed himself remained, hoping that thus he might turn the wrath of the idolaters upon himself and protect the flight of his children.

Presently, however, came information that forty men, one from each tribe, had sworn together to take his life; and forthwith Mohammed with Abu Bekr, his devoted friend, departed one dark night and shook off the dust of Mecca from his feet. Danger was so near that they dared not take the path to Medina, but made their way to a mountain, on whose rocky summit they found a small cave into which they crept at dawn of day.

Knowing what the end of the pursuit would mean, Abu began to lose nerve, and asked, "What if our pursuers should find our cave? We are but two."

"We are three," was the calm reply: "Allah is with us!"

Legend says that the pursuers actually approached the mouth of the cave and were about to investigate it. But in the early hours of the day Allah had caused a tree to grow up before it, a spider to weave its web across it, and a wild pigeon, most timid of birds, to lay eggs in a nest made in the branches; and the searchers, seeing these things, declared it impossible that any one could be within. A faithful friend provided them in secret with food and milk, and on the third night they began the journey to Medina.

"He is come! He is come!" cried the Faithful in Medina, flocking to meet the wayworn travellers as they entered the city.

And thus a new chapter was opened in the history of Islam.

CHAPTER II

Mohammed as Conqueror

He is come to ope
The purple testament of bleeding war.

SHAKESPEARE: *Richard II.*

The year which marked Mohammed's triumphant entry into Medina is known in the Mohammedan world as the *Hegira*, and counts as the Year One in their calendar—the year from which all others are reckoned. For the first time the faith of Islam was preached openly, and the claim of Mohammed to be merely *one* of the "prophets" gave place to a demand for acknowledgment as the chief of all, a demand calculated to arouse the antagonism of all other existing forms of religion. The other important development of his teaching at this time was that all faithful Moslems—the followers of the Prophet—must entirely abstain from the use of intoxicating drink.

Moreover, though at first Mohammed (possibly to please the Jews in Medina) had commanded that at the hour of prayer every Moslem should turn his face towards Jerusalem, in course of time, when he began to see the impossibility of uniting the Jewish believers with those of Islam, he suddenly, after the usual prostration, turned towards the Temple at Mecca. From that moment down to the present day the Moslem, wherever he is, follows this example at the fivefold hour of prayer.

At Medina, Mohammed married the young girl Ayesha, and, as permitted by the Moslem faith, soon brought other wives to the simply built house by the mosque which he and his converts were building just outside the city. Yet, though a man of fifty-three, the Prophet by no means intended to pass the rest of his life in ease and domestic comfort. He had been forced by violence to flee from Mecca. He now conceived it his duty to make himself master of his native city by means of the sword.

The sons of the desert are born fighters, and whether his motive was to enforce the Moslem faith at the peril of the sword, or merely to assert his personal rights, the fact remains that he had no difficulty whatever in rallying to his standard a small though most enthusiastic army.

An attempt to seize a rich caravan belonging to a merchant of Mecca was the signal for battle. The forces of Mecca, hastily gathered, went out against the Moslem host, and, after hard fighting, were dispersed. There was joy in Medina when the "swift dromedary" of the Prophet appeared at the house of prayer and the news was made known; but in Mecca was bitter hatred and woe, fitly expressed in the grim words of the wife of the slain leader of the caravan: "Not till ye again wage war against Mohammed and his fellows shall tears flow from my eyes! If tears would wash away grief, I would now weep, even as ye; but with me it is not so!"

From that time Mohammed gave up all pretence of winning converts by peaceable methods; henceforth he was to live and die a man of the sword. Deterioration of character was a more or less natural outcome of this change. It may have been necessary to invent visions in order to convince the ignorant people of Medina that their victory was due, not to their own strength, but to the aid of the angels of Allah, who would always fight upon their side; but we cannot say the same of the applause, given openly by Mohammed in the mosque, to the cold-blooded murderer of a woman who had composed some verses throwing doubt upon the right of the Prophet to glory in the death of the men of his own tribe. Nor was this the only instance of revenge and cruelty. It was but too clear that Mohammed, from a calm and peaceful prophet, had been transformed into a warlike chieftain, bent on subduing all others to his will. When Mecca declared battle, he went out to the field, clad in full armour, sword in hand. At first all went well with the Moslems. Then Mohammed was struck in the mouth and cheek, and a cry went up, "The Prophet is slain! Where is now the promise of Allah?" Their cry was drowned in the triumphant shouts of the men of Mecca, "War hath its revenge; Allah is for us—not for you!"

The day was lost; and it needed all the Prophet's ingenuity to account for it satisfactorily to those whom he had so often assured of the certain protection of Allah. From that time possibly dates the belief of the Moslems that he who dies in battle against the unbeliever is so certain of the joys of Paradise that it is the survivor rather than the slain who should be pitied.

Meantime, before the contest with Mecca could be finally settled, Mohammed undertook to crush, once for all, the Jewish power in Arabia. It seems strange that there should have been such hostility between Jews and Moslems, seeing that both claimed the God of Abraham as the object of their worship; but this was now lost sight of in view of the natural refusal of the former to acknowledge Mohammed as the chief of all prophets, and his sacred book, the Koran, as superior to their "Book of the Law," the Old Testament. By dint of persecuting those who dwelt within the walls of Medina, and of besieging their cities elsewhere, Mohammed compelled the Jews to migrate to Syria, leaving their abandoned lands and cities to him. The event finds special mention in the Koran.

"Allah it is who drove out the People of the Book, *(the Jews)*, who believed not, to join the former exiles. Ye thought not they would go forth; verily, *they* thought that their fortresses would defend them against Allah; but Allah came upon them from a quarter unexpected and covered their hearts with dread."

Soon after this event, Ali, his faithful nephew, was still more closely united with Mohammed by his marriage with Fatima, the Prophet's daughter; and thus he of whom Mohammed was wont to say, "I am the city of wisdom, but Ali is its door," was joined to one of the "four perfect women" spoken of by the Prophet.

It was now six years since Mohammed had left Mecca, during which time he had never ceased to yearn and plan for his triumphant return. The Kaaba, save for its idols, was sacred to him as the home of the worship of Allah, and his heart was bitter within him when he reflected that he and his followers had been so long forbidden the yearly pilgrimage thither. So he determined to put the temper of the Meccans to the test by making a pilgrimage, with a sufficient number of followers to resist any aggressive act of hostility. As they approached the sacred borders, the camel of Mohammed refused to go further. "The creature is obstinate and weary," said the Moslems. "Not so," answered Mohammed, "the hand of Allah restrains her. If the Meccans make any demand of me this day, I will grant it. Let the caravan halt." "There is no water here," they cried in dismay, "how shall we halt?" But Mohammed ordered that a dried-up well should be opened, and at once water bubbled up to the surface.

Still more surprised were the Moslems, all of whom were burning to fight, when they found the Prophet quietly accepting the terms offered by the men of Mecca, when they promised to permit future pilgrimages, though they would not allow him to enter the city on that occasion.

Once recognised by his own birthplace, Mohammed determined to bring about his most ambitious project, and to summon all the kingdoms of the earth to acknowledge Islam.

He even had a signet-ring engraved with the words "Mohammed, the Apostle of Allah," and, in a spirit of sublime self-confidence, sent it to the King of Persia, to the Byzantine Emperor Heraclius, and to the rulers of Syria, Abyssinia, and Egypt. Nothing came of it, of course, and meantime the earlier desire of his heart had been gratified. The pilgrimage to Mecca had been undertaken in safety, and the Prophet had worshipped after the manner of Islam within the very walls of the sacred Kaaba.

That same year saw the Moslems on the march against the forces of Rome herself. One of the Prophet's envoys had been put to death by the Christian chieftain of a Syrian tribe, which was under Roman rule; and the little Moslem army at once set out from Medina to avenge him. Little did Mohammed know of the Roman military power when he sent forth his men with such high words of courage. The Moslem troops advanced, crying "Paradise! how fair is thy resting-place! Cold is the water there and sweet the shade! Rome! Rome! The hour of thy woe draweth nigh! When we close with her, we shall hurl her to the dust."

Instead of this, a discomfited rabble made their way back to Medina in hot haste, to be received with cries of "Oh, runaways! Do ye indeed flee before the enemy when fighting for Allah?"

Nor did the conquest of several wandering desert tribes soothe the wounded pride of the Prophet. He could only be consoled by his next project of making himself master of Mecca, the Holy City, itself. He was strong enough now to put ten thousand of his followers in the field, and with these, after a rapid and secret march, he encamped on the hills above the city, where his ten thousand twinkling watch-fires could strike terror into the hearts of the inhabitants. That night a chieftain of the men of Mecca, going forth in the darkness to reconnoitre the enemy, was captured and brought before the Prophet. Threatened with death, he agreed to embrace the faith of Islam, and was forthwith sent back to his city with this message:—

"Every Meccan who is found in thy dwelling; all who take refuge in the Kaaba; and whosoever shutteth the door of his own house upon his family, shall be safe: haste thee home!"

The army followed hard upon his heels, fearing treachery; but the new-made convert kept faith; and when they entered Mecca, it was like a city of the dead.

The first act of Mohammed was to destroy the idols in the Kaaba, and to sound the call for prayer from its summit. But except in the case of a few rebellious spirits, no blood was shed, and no cruelty shown to those who had once been his persecutors. The chiefs of the Meccans indeed came before him, fearing the worst; and of them he asked, "What can you expect at my hands?"

"Mercy, O generous brother," they answered.

"Be it so; ye are free!" was the Prophet's reply.

"Thus, after an exile of seven years, the fugitive missionary was enthroned as the Prince and Prophet of his native country."

In the years that followed his triumphant possession of Mecca, all the tribes and cities from the Euphrates to the head of the Red Sea submitted to Mohammed, who thus became the founder of a new empire as well as of a new religion. Many of these tribes were Christian, and to them the Prophet always showed the utmost kindness and toleration for their worship. As the enemies of the hated Jews they had a special claim on his favour; and it was no doubt to his own advantage to be on good terms with a religion destined to be the most powerful in the world.

During the last four years of his life the strength of the Prophet began to flag under the incessant demands made upon it. He was now over sixty years of age, and, just as he was proposing to undertake a new raid into Roman territory, he was attacked by a high fever. Recovering for a time, he appeared once more in the mosque at the time of prayer. Returning to his couch, his great and increasing weakness warned him that the end was near.

"O God, pardon my sins!" he faltered. "Yes—I come—among my fellow-citizens on high."

Thus he died, in the tenth year after the Hegira.

CHAPTER III

The Spread of Islam

Swift and resistless through the land he passed,
Like that bold Greek who did the East subdue,
And made to battles such heroic haste
As if on wings of victory he flew.

DRYDEN: *On Cromwell.*

Of those sovereigns visited by the envoys of Mohammed and bidden to give their allegiance to the Prophet, was Khosru, King of Persia, who, in utter disdain of such a demand, tore the letter to pieces.

"Beware, O king," said the messenger as he departed, "for in the days to come your kingdom shall be treated as you have treated the written words of the Prophet."

The idea of an unknown sect from an Arabian desert attacking the power of the "Great King" seemed preposterous to those who heard, for Persia was then at the height of one of her spasmodic periods of success. Some eighteen years before the envoy of Islam appeared at his court the king had covered his empire with glory by the capture of Jerusalem (611 A.D.), then in the hands of Rome, and inhabited chiefly by Christians. On this occasion the Jews throughout Palestine rose on his behalf with the object of exterminating the Christians, ninety thousand of whom are said to have perished. "Every Christian church was demolished, that of the Holy Sepulchre was the object of furious hatred; the stately building of Helena and Constantine was abandoned to the flames; the devout offerings of three hundred years were rifled in one sacrilegious day." Fortunately for future ages, the great church, built by the pious Helena over the place where the body of Christ had lain, was not entirely destroyed; but—a worse blow still to the Christian inhabitants—the True Cross was taken from its sacred hiding place and carried Into Persia.

Egypt had also fallen into the hands of the conquering Khosru, when at length Heraclius, the Emperor of the East, "slumbering on the throne of Constantinople," awoke, drove the Persian from Syria and Egypt, restored the ruined churches of Jerusalem, and brought back in triumph the Cross to the Holy City.

The preceding year had seen the fall of Khosru, and peace concluded between the Empires of Rome and Persia; eight years later Jerusalem was in the hands of the Saracens (637 A.D.).

The years intervening between this event and the death of Mohammed had been utilised by the sons of Islam in making a series of conquests, which seem well-nigh miraculous. We can indeed only account for them by the fact that the contest was between a race of fighters, stirred by their new faith to a perfect frenzy of enthusiasm, and the remnants of Empires far gone in decay.

Yet, even so, there was no light task. Chaldaea and Babylonia, perhaps the most ancient empires in the world, fell before the sword of Islam only after a long and terrible struggle. The bloodshed on both sides was appalling, but the ever-increasing numbers of Moslems were always providing fresh recruits, eager to win victory or Paradise. Even when they were less numerous than their enemies, they more than made up for it by the determination and obstinacy of their attacks.

Emboldened by this success, the Saracens flung themselves upon the Empire of Persia. Three months after the great battle of Cadesia, the "white palace" of Khosru was in their hands, and the remnants of the Persian hosts had fled before them.

The story of Harmozan, the Prince of Susa, Persia's most important city, shows the craft of the native Persian, and the binding nature of the Islamite promise. Brought before Omar the Caliph of Islam, stripped of his gorgeous robes, bullied and insulted, Harmozan complained of intolerable thirst. They brought him a cup of water, which he eyed askance.

"What ails the man?" cried Omar. "I fear, my lord, lest I be killed even as I drink," confessed Harmozan. "Be of good courage," replied the Caliph, "your life is safe till you have drunk the water." Instantly the crafty ruler dashed the cup to the ground, and when Omar would have avenged his deceit, the bystanders promptly reminded him that the word of a Moslem is as sacred as an oath. Harmozan was liberated, and became speedily a convert to a religion which taught so well how to "keep faith."

While these conquests were being made in the East, the forces of Omar had been making equal progress in the West.

Palestine was their destination, and Damascus, that famous city, the centre of immense trade, their first prey.

From thence they advanced upon Jerusalem, taking town after town on the way. A siege of four months convinced the Christian Patriarch that it was hopeless to hold out longer. All he now demanded was that Omar himself should come to take possession, on the ground that it was written in the sacred book of the Jews that the city should one day fall into the hands of a king having but four letters in his name.

In Arabia the word "Omar" fulfilled this condition, and forthwith the Caliph arrived, in the plainest garb, riding upon a camel, and bearing with him his pouch of grain and dates and his skin of water.

To meet him came the chieftains he had sent out two years before, clad in the rich cloths of Damascus.

"Is it thus ye come before me?" cried Omar in disgust, throwing a handful of sand in their faces. Dismayed for a moment, they recollected themselves, and, opening their gorgeous robes, revealed the armour beneath.

"Enough!" cried the Caliph. "Go forward!"

The terms arranged were by no means harsh, though clearly marking the inferior position of the conquered Christians. No crosses were to be shown, nor church bells rung in the street. A

Christian must rise and stand in the presence of a Moslem. The latter might practise his religion and use his church undisturbed; but the great mosque of Omar was to rise over the ruined altar of the temple and over the sacred stone upon which the patriarch Jacob had once rested his head.

Strange as it may seem, the two races settled down side by side in peace and friendship. Both acknowledged the holiness of the Israelites of old, whose bones lay buried in the neighbourhood of the Holy City. Within its walls the Mohammedans treated with respect, if not with reverence, the worship of Him whom they regarded as a prophet not far inferior to their own. Thus four centuries rolled quietly away, until the old distinction between conquerors and conquered had almost ceased to exist, and pilgrims from all parts of Christendom were welcomed by Christian and Moslem alike.

Meantime the forces of Islam threatened to overrun the greater part of the known world. The Saracens "rode masters of the sea," throughout the Greek archipelago; their sway was recognised towards the East up to the sources of the Euphrates and Tigris, to the North they had spread over Asia Minor deep to the very walls of Constantinople, the seat of the Eastern Empire.

Egypt was conquered by Amrou, one of the most famous generals of the Caliph Omar. With Egypt fell Alexandria, a city renowned for its learning, and especially for its magnificent library, through the civilised world.

"I have taken," Amrou told the Caliph, "the great city of the West. It contains four thousand palaces, four thousand baths, four hundred theatres or places of amusement, twelve thousand shops for the sale of vegetable food, and forty thousand tributary Jews. The town has been subdued by force of arms, without treaty or capitulation, and the Moslems are impatient to seize the fruits of their victory."

Fortunately for the inhabitants, who were the last to be referred to, Omar would not allow slaughter or pillage. But if the tale be true, the fate of the famous library of Alexandria shows very clearly the narrow limits of Saracen culture in those days.

A learned scholar of the city, who had won the liking and respect of Amrou, entreated that the library might be given over to him, as the Moslems would have no use for it. The question was referred to Omar, who replied, "If these writings of the Greeks agree with the Book of God, they are useless, and need not be preserved; if they disagree, they are harmful, and should be destroyed." And forthwith the priceless volumes were committed to the flames.

Six years later (647 A.D.) the warrior Othman accomplished the conquest of Northern Africa; and a little more than sixty years later, a small expedition of Saracens crossed the Straits of Gibraltar and set foot in Spain. Their leader, Tarif, gave his name to the place (Tarifa) where he landed, and likewise to the "tariff" or "duty" levied upon the vessels which passed through the straits.

At Xeres they were met by Roderick, the "last of the Goths," who was killed, and whose army was put to flight by the forces of the Saracens, or Moors as they were called after their settlement in Mauretania or Morocco, just across the straits. But the conquest of Spain by the Moors, teeming as it is with romantic interest, is too long to be related here, and we must retrace our steps to the East.

By the end of the first half of the eighth century, and only a little over a hundred years after Mohammed's death, the Saracens had brought their career of conquest almost to an end, and were firmly established as "the most potent and absolute monarchs of the globe." One determined attempt, indeed, was made during the latter half of the century to take Constantinople, the capital of the Eastern Empire. A battle was fought beneath the walls of the city, and the Saracens were victorious; but they were prevailed upon to retire on the promise of an immense yearly tribute.

The beginning of the ninth century saw the Eastern and Western worlds ruled respectively by those two famous monarchs of history and romance, Haroun-Al-Raschid and Charlemagne. The first is familiar to most of us through the enchanting pages of the *Arabian Nights*, but history unfortunately gives us a darker portrait of the renowned Caliph, painting him as a jealous and selfish tyrant. He was, however, a patron of literature and of art, which distinguishes him from his predecessors, who were merely warriors. He could fight, too, on occasion, both with tongue and sword. A new

Emperor of Constantinople chose to refuse the tribute promised by the late Empress in these words.

"Nicephorus, King of the Greeks, to Haroun, King of the Arabs.

"The late Queen was too humble; she submitted to pay tribute to you, though she should have exacted twice as much from you. A man speaks to you now; therefore send back the tribute you have received, otherwise the sword shall be umpire between me and thee."

The Caliph replied in unmistakable terms—

"In the name of Allah, most merciful!"

"Haroun-al-Raschid, Commander of the Faithful, to Nicephorus, the Roman dog.

"I have read thy letter, O thou son of an unbelieving mother! Thou shalt not hear, but thou shalt see my reply."

Forthwith a huge force crossed over into the domains of Nicephorus, and only the promise to pay the tribute twice, instead of once a year, induced the Caliph to withdraw his forces.

To us, however, the most interesting incident of his reign is the link that was forged between East and West when the great Haroun courteously received the ambassadors of Charlemagne at his court in Bagdad. He may have been prompted only by a desire to obtain the Great Emperor of the West as his ally against the Emperor of the Eastern Empire, but there seems little doubt that Haroun actually sent to Charlemagne the keys of the Holy Places at Jerusalem, declaring that the city belonged first and foremost to the Champion of Christendom.

Pilgrim's of the XIth Century journeying to the Holy City   41

Pilgrims of the XIth Century journeying to the Holy City

Charlemagne did not hesitate to avail himself of this generosity. Fifty years later, a monk of Brittany, named Bernard the Wise, described how he was lodged at the hospital of the most glorious Emperor Charles, wherein are received all pilgrims who speak Latin, and who come for a religious reason. There, too, he discovered the fine library founded by Charlemagne close by, in the Church of the Blessed Virgin. He speaks in high terms of the relations existing between Christians and Moslems, both at Jerusalem and in Egypt.

"The Christians and Pagans," he says, "have there such peace between them that, if I should go a journey, and in this journey my camel or ass which carried my burdens should die, and I should leave everything there without a guard, and go to the next town to get another, on my return I should find all my property untouched."

Thus, in peace and security, the long stream of pilgrims from the West flowed towards the Holy City until the beginning of the eleventh century. Then came, quite suddenly, a terrible interval of persecution. The reigning Caliph, El Hakim, became, as he grew up, a fierce and fanatical madman. Inflamed, it is said, by the report of the Jews, who warned him that unless he put a stop to the crowds of pilgrims he would soon find himself without a kingdom, he instituted a fierce persecution of the Christians, and commanded that the Church of the Holy Sepulchre should be destroyed. Another furious outburst was directed against the Jews themselves, as well as the Christians. Many were killed, and many of their churches laid low.

Just before his end a fit of remorse seized El Hakim, and he commanded that the churches of the Christians should be restored. Before he could again change his mind, he was assassinated by command of his own sister, as being a dangerous madman.

A brief interval of toleration followed, which was but the lull before the storm; for an outbreak of terrible persecution was to come, an outbreak which was the immediate cause of the First Crusade.

CHAPTER IV

The Rise of Chivalry

A knight there was, and that a worthy man,
That fro the tyme that he first began
To riden out, he loved chivalrie,
Trouthe and honour, freedom and curteisie.

CHAUCER: *The Prologue.*

During the interval of comparative peace that followed the downfall of the mad Caliph Hakim, a new spirit of religious devotion began to awaken in Christendom.

This was, to a large extent, a reaction from a truly "dark age"—the period which immediately preceded the end of the tenth century. Famine and pestilence had devastated Europe, and had resulted in absolute demoralisation of the population. Travellers went their way in fear not only of robbery, but of a far worse fate. It was whispered that men, women and children had been waylaid in forest depths, torn to pieces, and devoured alive by human wild beasts. The Church, in her efforts to bring about a better state of things, resorted to counsels of despair, and began to preach, in every part of Christendom, that the end of the world was at hand, and that the appointed time was the thousandth year after the birth of Christ.

The result was an outburst of intense religious excitement which did much to check the progress of evil and outrage. It had a practical outcome, too, as is seen in that curious institution known as the Truce of God. In joining this, every knight took an oath not to commit sacrilege; to treat all travellers with respect; to "keep the peace" during the sacred days of each week—that is, from Wednesday evening to Monday morning; not to fight for purposes of private revenge, and always to defend and keep sacred the persons of women. Here we have clearly the foundation of that spirit of chivalry which plays such a prominent part in the Story of the Crusades.

The appointed time for the end of the world came and went, but the spirit of devotion remained. A new interest was awakened in the scenes of the life-work of the Saviour, and crowds of pilgrims, young and old, of all ranks and professions, hastened to undertake the long and toilsome journey to the Holy Land.

Many of these suffered under the persecution of Hakim; and even after his time, though no active measures were taken against them, they were not received with the favour shown in former days. But this only added zest to the enterprise. To visit the Church of the Holy Tomb, and to return and build a church in his own land, became the ambition of every man of wealth and high rank; while the poor palmer, with his staff and hat decorated with palm sprigs or cockle-shells, became a well-known figure upon the roads of every country in Europe.

Says a writer of that day, "At the time there begun to flow towards the Holy Sepulchre so great a multitude as, ere this, no man could have hoped for. First of all went the poorer folk, then men of middle rank, and lastly, very many kings and counts, marquises and bishops; aye, and a thing that had never happened before, many women bent their steps in the same direction."

Things were made a little easier for them by the conversion of the Huns to Christianity; for this enabled the pilgrims to pass along the land route through Hungary instead of crossing the Mediterranean and travelling through Egypt.

Robert the Magnificent, the father of William, the future "Conqueror," was among these eleventh century pilgrims, and he, like many another, died before he could return home.

Sweyn, the eldest and worst of the sons of Godwin, was another; and Eldred, Bishop of York in the days of William the Conqueror, made the little realm of England famous at Jerusalem by his gift before the Holy Sepulchre of a wonderful golden chalice.

Side by side with this spirit of religious zeal there grew up and developed that remarkable body of sentiment and custom known as chivalry.

Chivalry has been described as the "whole duty of a gentleman"; and when we realise the condition of barbarism, brutality, and vice out of which even Western Christendom was only just emerging in the eleventh century, we can see how important was the work it had to do. Religion, Honour, Courtesy—those were the three watchwords of the knight of chivalry, and they covered a wide area of conduct.

The education of a knight began at the age of seven, and commenced with the personal service, which was regarded in those days as a privilege. The small boy was proud to hold the wine-cup behind the chair of his lord, or his stirrup when he rode on horseback. For the next seven years, though much of his time was spent in waiting upon the ladies of the household, who taught him reading, writing, music, and the laws of chivalry, he also learnt the duties of a squire—how to hunt and hawk, and to look after the kennels and the stables. At the age of fourteen the boy might be called a squire, when his duty, in addition to those mentioned, would be to carve for his lord at table, tasting the food first himself for fear of poison; and also, of course, to attend upon him at all times. Thus he had to arm him for battle, to see that his weapons were in perfect condition, to fight by his side, and to lie before his door while he slept.

When the squire had mastered all his duties and obligations, he had then to "win his spurs," that is, to perform some deed of valour that should prove him worthy of knighthood.

The ceremony of girding on his armour was largely a religious one. The whole of the previous night was spent by him on his knees with his sword held upright between his hands, before the altar upon which his armour was laid. Thus he dedicated himself by prayer and fasting to the service of God, and on the morrow was solemnly consecrated by the Church to his high office, before the armour was actually buckled on.

This last part of the ceremony was the privilege of some fair damsel, to whom the knight was bound to give devotion and respect. "To do the pleasure of ladies was his chief solace and the mainspring of his service."

Another of the features of chivalry was that of "brotherhood-in-arms," by which two knights vowed eternal faith and love to one another. They dressed alike, wore similar armour, prayed together, supported each other in battle and in any kind of quarrel, and had the same friends and enemies.

That their devotion to the rules of chivalry was a very real thing is proved over and over again by the conduct of the knights who took part in the Crusades. It is well expressed by Tristan, in one of the most famous romances of the chivalric age. As he lay dying, he said to his squire, "I take leave of chivalry which I have so much loved and honoured. Alas! my sword, what wilt thou do now? Wilt thou hear, Sagremor, the most shameful word that ever passed the lips of Tristan? I am conquered. I give thee my arms, I give thee my chivalry."

It took many a long year to bring to perfection this great institution, with all its rules and regulations, and chivalry was but in its infancy when the First Crusade began. The two movements developed together, and many a chivalric lesson was learnt by the knights of Christendom from the Moslems of the East. Perhaps, however, one of the most marked effects of the Crusades upon this greatest of mediæval institutions was the welding together of the various nations of Europe in a common knighthood, bound by the same rules and codes of honour, and fighting for the same cause.

"All wars and brigandage came to an end. The Crusade, like the rain, stilled the wind."

Out of this combination of the spirit of chivalry, with that of the Crusades themselves, sprang certain military orders, which play a very prominent part in the history of the time.

The first of these was known as the Order of the Knights Hospitallers. About the middle of the eleventh century a guest-house or "hospital," where pilgrims could be entertained, was established by a company of Italian merchants, in connection with the Church of St Mary, opposite that of the Holy Sepulchre, in Jerusalem. This hospital, dedicated to St John, was managed by Benedictine monks, under one called the "Guardian of the Redeemer's Poor." When the First Crusade was over, its hero, Godfrey of Boulogne, visited the place and found that these good monks had devoted themselves during the siege of Jerusalem to the care of the sick and wounded Christians, giving them the best of all they possessed, and living themselves in the utmost poverty. Godfrey at once endowed the Hospital of St John with lands and money, and set up one Gerard as its first Grand Master. A new and splendid church was built for the monks, and a habit or dress was prescribed for their use, consisting of a black robe with a cross of eight points in white linen upon it—the famous Maltese Cross of later days.

Early in the twelfth century, this company of priests and holy laymen was changed by its second Grand Master into a military order, bound to carry on the same kind of charitable work in tending the sick and wounded, but specially to defend the Holy Sepulchre by force of arms. Many of this order of "Brothers" had been originally knights who had retired from the world and taken religious vows; hence it was said that the changes merely "gave back to the brethren the arms that they had quitted." These were now distinguished from the rest by a red surcoat with the white cross worn over armour.

Except for the obligation of fighting the vows were not changed, and these Knights Hospitallers owed the same allegiance to the three-fold laws of obedience, chastity, and poverty as ordinary monks. The brethren were to be the "servants of the poor"; no member could call anything his own; he might not marry; he could use arms only against the Saracen; but he was independent of any authority save that of the Pope.

This Order became immensely popular; in the thirteenth century it numbered fifteen thousand knights, many of them drawn from the noblest houses of Christendom; and it is much to its credit that, at a time when chivalry had become little more than a name, it upheld the old traditions even when it had been driven from Palestine, and forced to find a new home for itself at Rhodes. Driven from thence in the sixteenth century, the Knights of St John were settled by the Emperor Charles V. at Malta, where they remained until the days of the French Revolution.

The Order of the Knights Templars was founded early in the twelfth century by Baldwin, then King of Jerusalem, as a "perpetual sacred soldiery," whose special object was to defend the Holy Sepulchre and the passes infested by brigands which led the pilgrims to Jerusalem. Their headquarters was a building granted them by Baldwin, close to the temple on Mt. Moriah. War was their first and most important business, though they were bound by their rule to a certain amount of prayer and fasting. The latter was, however, easily relaxed, and "to drink like a Templar" became a proverb.

In every battle of the Holy War these two Orders took a prominent part; the post of honour on the right being claimed by the Templars, that on the left by the Hospitallers. Unlike most other knights, the Templars wore long beards, and from their dress of white, with a large red cross upon it, they gained the title of the Red-Cross Knights.

You will, no doubt, remember that Spenser's knight in the first book of the Faery Queene was of that order.

And on his breast a bloudy cross he bore
In dear remembrance of his dying lord.

Their banner was half black, half white; "fair and favourable to the friends of Christ, black and terrible to His foes."

These Knights Templars, by their arrogance and independence, made for themselves many enemies, and early in the fourteenth century they were strongly opposed by Philip of France. By this time they were established in various parts of Europe, and one of their most powerful "houses" was the building known as the "Temple" in Paris, the members of which openly defied the authority of the king.

With some difficulty the consent of a weak Pope was obtained for their destruction. On a given day, when the Grand Master and most of his knights were staying in France, every Templar in the country was seized, imprisoned, and tortured until he had confessed crimes, many of which he probably had never imagined in his wildest moments. More than five hundred were burnt alive, as a preliminary to the Order being declared extinct. Whether the Templars deserved their terrible fate may well be a matter of doubt, though public opinion, in their own day, was decidedly against them. It is generally considered that Philip's treatment of an order, the members of which had again and again laid down their lives for the cause of God, ranks as one of the blackest crimes of history.

There is a legend to the effect that on each anniversary of the suppression of the Order, the heads of seven of the martyred Templars rise from their graves to meet a phantom figure clad in the red-cross mantle. The latter cries three times, "Who shall now defend the Holy Temple? Who shall free the Sepulchre of the Lord?"

And the seven heads make mournful reply, "None! The Temple is destroyed."

The Temple Church, in London, was originally built for the English branch of this great Order, the members of which in England, as well as in Spain and Germany, were almost all acquitted of the charges brought against them.

But we must now return to the period prior to the foundation of these two great Orders, with which are associated most of the gallant deeds of the Holy War.

CHAPTER V

The Story of Peter the Hermit

Great troops of people travelled thitherward
Both day and night, of each degree and place
But Jew returned, having 'scaped hard
With hateful beggary or foul disgrace.

SPENSER: *Faery Queene.*

Some twenty years after the death of Hakim, the countries round about the Holy Land began to be harassed by a new and terrible foe. From far-off Turkestan had migrated a fierce fighting tribe, the descendants of one Seljuk, and known to history as the Seljukian Turks. Wherever they went they conquered, until half-way through the eleventh century, their leader drove out the Saracen rulers of Bagdad and made himself Caliph.

His successor was converted to Islam, and with added power, swept over Asia Minor and settled in the city of Nicæa, in threatening proximity to Constantinople.

This invasion was the more terrible in that it brought in its train a relapse to barbarism, for these Turks were barbarians, hordes of robbers and brigands, who cared for nothing but plunder and violence.

Alexios, the weak Emperor of the Eastern Empire, quailed at their approach, and looked on in terror at the spectacle of Christian churches destroyed and Christian children sold into slavery. But he appealed in vain for aid to the kingdom of the West. To unite Western Christendom against a far-off foe was a task beyond the powers of the tottering Empire of the East.

That inspiration, however, was at hand. In 1076, the Seljukian Turks conquered Jerusalem, and at once began a reign of terror for

Christian inhabitants and pilgrims. The Patriarch, or Bishop of Jerusalem, was dragged through the street by his white hair, and flung into a dungeon, until his people could gather a sum sufficient to pay his ransom. The holiest sacrament of the Church was profaned by the barbarians, who invaded the buildings and insisted upon sharing in the rite. Pilgrims were stripped and beaten on the roads and passes that led to the Holy City; many suffered martyrdom as they knelt before the Holy Tomb. Out of seven thousand who set out from Germany in one year, only two thousand returned to tell a tale of cruel murder and outrage. The marvel is that such a terrible state of things was allowed to exist so long, without anything being done to remedy it. Pope Gregory VII. (Hildebrand) did indeed gather an army in the latter part of the eleventh century, but his energy was dissipated in the hopeless task of asserting the power of the Pope over the Emperor, and his army was eventually dispersed.

Robert Guiscard, the Norman, actually crossed the sea with his troops in 1081, when death overtook him; and for a time the unhappy pilgrims seemed to be left to their fate. Then suddenly was heard a "voice calling in the wilderness," the voice of one who was to be the herald of the First Crusade.

The story goes that a certain poor hermit named Peter, a native of the French city of Amiens, set out to go to Jerusalem in the year 1098. He had, like every one else, heard of the horrors he might be called upon to endure, but pushed on, undeterred, until, possibly because of his poverty, he arrived safely within the Holy City. He found the condition of things even worse than he expected. The very stones of the great church were stained with the blood of the martyrs; the cries of tortured women rang in his ears; the patriarch Simeon confessed that he had lost heart and was little better than a slave in the Moslem's hands. It was clear that the Emperor of the East, their proper protector, would never act up to his responsibilities. To whom, then, could they look for aid?

"The nations of the West shall take up arms in your cause," cried the dauntless Peter, and he forthwith promised to visit the Pope and obtain his help and sympathy on his return journey, if the Patriarch would give him letters to the Church of Rome.

That night, says the legend, Peter meant to spend in watching at the tomb of the Saviour, and there he fell asleep. And as he slept, the figure of the Redeemer stood before him, and with hand outstretched, bade him hasten to fulfil his great task, saying, "So shalt thou make known the woes of My people, and rouse the faithful to cleanse the Holy Places from the infidel; for through danger and trial of every kind shall the elect now enter the gates of Paradise."

With these words ringing in his ears, the Hermit at once hurried to the coast and sailed for Italy. He came before Pope Urban II. at the very time when the envoys of the Emperor of Constantinople were knocking very hard at the doors of Rome. Urban therefore did not hesitate to bless the enterprise of Peter, and to bid him go forth and preach a Crusade in his own way.

To induce kings, princes, and nobles, to leave their lands and go to fight in a cause from which they could gain no apparent profit, needed considerable time, and Urban himself undertook the difficult task. But he was wise enough to see that the peculiar power of Peter the Hermit could be used in stirring up the ordinary people, the simple-minded and the poor, to take up arms for the cause of Christ. So, as a writer of his own time puts it, "The hermit set out, from whence I know not, but we saw him passing through the towns and villages, preaching everywhere, and the people surrounding him in crowds, loading him with offerings and celebrating his sanctity with such great praises that I never remember such honour bestowed on any one."

Throughout Italy and France and along the banks of the Rhine journeyed the strange inspired figure, with head and feet bare, his thin frame wrapped in a coarse cloak, holding before him a great crucifix as he rode upon an ass.

"He preached to innumerable crowds in the churches, the streets and the highways; the Hermit entered with equal confidence the palace and the cottage; and the people were impetuously moved by his call to repentance and to arms. When he painted the sufferings of the natives and pilgrims of Palestine, every heart was melted to compassion; every breast glowed with indignation when he challenged the warriors of the age to defend their brethren and rescue their Saviour."

While Southern Europe was thus being stirred to enthusiasm by being brought into personal contact with one who had seen for himself the woes of the Holy Land, Pope Urban had already called a council to consider the matter in a practical form. At this Council of Placentia, however, the chief part of the attention of those present was drawn to the representations of the Greek Emperor, on whose behalf ambassadors pleaded the cause of the city of Constantinople. If that city fell before the threatened onslaught of the Turks, they said, Christianity must perish for ever in the East, and nothing but a narrow stretch of sea kept the Moslems from the gates of the capital city of the Eastern Empire.

At these words the deepest sympathy was expressed, but it was suggested that the best way of succouring the threatened city was to draw off the attention of the Turks by an attack upon Palestine itself. This was just what Urban desired. A definite march upon Jerusalem would fire the imaginations of men of all ranks far more than an attempt to defend Constantinople before it was actually besieged. The old jealousy between the Eastern and Western Empire had to be reckoned with; and the Emperor Alexios was no heroic figure to stand for the Cause of Christ. The whole question, was, therefore, deferred until the autumn of 1095, when a Council was summoned at Clermont in France.

That dull November day witnessed a most striking scene. The vast open square in front of the Cathedral was crammed with people of all classes drawn from all quarters by the rumour that the subject of a Crusade would be discussed. From the great western door, immediately after High Mass, emerged the figure of the Pope, and a number of bishops and cardinals, dressed in vestments glowing with colour, followed him upon the high scaffold covered with red cloth.

The Preaching of Peter the Hermit 59

The Preaching of Peter the Hermit

With cross outstretched in his left hand, the Pope held up his right to command attention, and then began to speak. "Who can preserve the force of that eloquence?" says one who stood by, and heard him point out that the Turks, having pushed their way to the edge of the Western World, and even then holding parts of Spain and Sicily, must now be driven forth from that holiest place, where Christianity alone had a right to enter.

Turning to the knights who stood by, leaning upon their swords, Urban addressed them in words of fire.

"Were they spending their days in empty quarrels, shearing their brethren like sheep? Let them go forth and fight boldly for the Cause of God. Christ himself would be their leader as, more valiant than the Israelites of old, they fought for their Jerusalem. A goodly thing would it be for them to die in that city, where Christ for them laid down His life. Let them, as valiant knights, descendants of unconquered sires, remember the vigour of their ancestors and go forth to conquer or to die."

This appeal stirred the multitude to its depths.

"DEUS VULT! DEUS VULT! (It is the will of God! It is the will of God!)

went up to heaven in one great roar of voices, and the cry was at once seized upon by Urban.

"Let these words be your war-cry," he exclaimed. "When you attack the enemy, let the words resound from every side, 'God wills it.' Go forth then; many sufferings will be yours, but you may redeem your souls at the expense of your bodies. Rid God's sanctuary of the wicked; expel the robbers; bring in the holy souls. These things I command, and for their carrying out I fix the end of next spring. If you have rich possessions here, you are promised better ones in the Holy Land. Those who die will enter the mansions of heaven, while the living shall behold the sepulchre of their Lord. Ye are soldiers of the Cross; wear then on your breasts, or on your shoulders, the blood-red sign of Him who died for the salvation of your souls. Wear it as a token that His help will never fail you; wear it as a pledge of a vow which can never be recalled."

Another mighty burst of applause followed these words.

Crowds of bishops and knights at once pressed forward to take the red cross badges which had been prepared, and Adhemar, Bishop of Puy, the first to do so, was at once appointed as spiritual head of the expedition, with Raymond, Count of Toulouse, as its military leader.

In the months that followed, all Southern Europe rang with the sounds of riveting armour and of forging steel. The actual departure of the Crusaders had been finally appointed for the August of 1090, but this was not early enough for the fervent spirits who had been already stirred to the depths by Peter the Hermit.

In the month of March, without preparation or provision for the journey, a vast concourse of some sixty thousand men and women turned their faces to the East, with Peter as their leader. As a writer of the time says, "Lands were deserted of their labourers; houses of their inhabitants; even whole cities migrated. You might see the husband departing with his wife, yea, with all his family, you would smile to see the whole household laden on a waggon, about to proceed on their journey. The road was too narrow for the passengers, the paths too hedged-in for the travellers, so thickly were they thronged by endless multitudes."

About fifteen thousand pilgrims, mostly French, assembled in this way at Cologne, about Easter 1096; and finding Peter unwilling to start before the German contingent had come up, they set off under a leader known as Walter the Penniless, and made for Constantinople. To do this they had to pass through Hungary, a wild and barren tract, the people of which had only lately been converted to Christianity; and here the rough discipline which Walter, by mere force of character, had managed to impose upon the horde that followed him, entirely broke down. Food being denied them, the pilgrims began to plunder. The Hungarians at once took up arms, and soon scattered the so-called troops in all directions. Hundreds took refuge in a church, which was promptly fired, and most of those within were burnt to death. Only a few thousand managed to hide in the woods and so escape; and this poor remnant, being collected with pain and difficulty by Walter the Penniless, made their way to Constantinople and put themselves under the protection of the Emperor until Peter should arrive.

Meantime, the Hermit had started, with a German following of about forty thousand people. Amongst these were quite a large number of women and children, many of whom doubtless did their part by cheering and helping their men-folk on the long road. But the hardships of the way told heavily on them, many fell out and lingered behind, beseeching the men to wait for them. Long forced marches were an impossibility, and a disorderly progress was made, in spite of the fact that they had more provisions and more money than their predecessors on the road.

At length they came to the spot where so many of Walter's followers had lost their lives. The place was but too well marked out by the weapons and crosses of the pilgrims which now adorned the walls and houses of the neighbouring town. In a wild outburst of fury, the mob threw itself upon the inhabitants, all unsuspecting as they were, and massacred them by the thousand. Enraged at this treatment of his people, the Hungarian King came down upon them with his forces, just as the pilgrims were endeavouring to cross the river into Bulgaria, and many perished before they could escape.

Once again, in crossing through Bulgaria, the undisciplined host came to blows with their fellow-Christians living in those lands. In vain did Peter represent that valuable lives, time and money was being wasted. About ten thousand lost their lives. Peter himself barely escaped to a wood, where he wandered about all night in misery, thinking that all his host was slain. Next day, however, he managed to collect about seven thousand, and as he marched on, other refugees joined him, until at length he found himself at the head of about half the force with which he had set out. Famished and gaunt, having lost nearly all the women and children, as well as food, clothes and money, Peter hurried them on till at length quite exhausted, they reached the walls of Constantinople.

Here they found the remnant of the army of Walter the Penniless, who had, from the first, kept his men under better control than had the Hermit. It was only too clear, however, that neither army was in a fit state to carry on a difficult warfare with the fighting Turks.

The Emperor Alexios, therefore, persuaded them to rest and recruit until the organised Crusading Army should appear, meantime giving them all they could require, and treating them with the greatest kindness.

But it seemed as though a curse, instead of a blessing, rested upon these forerunners of the First Crusade.

The pilgrims became quite unruly, burnt the houses of their hosts, stripped the lead from some of the churches and actually tried to sell it to the inhabitants of the city. The Greeks naturally turned against their ill-mannered guests, and Alexios, dreading the consequences, persuaded Peter to take them with him over the Bosphorus into Asia Minor.

Thankful for his aid in transporting them, Peter got his men across the strait, but, all too soon after they had encamped on the other side, a fresh quarrel broke out between the followers of Walter and those of Peter. Utterly unable to control his own men, Peter threw up his task and retired to Constantinople alone.

Freed from all pretence of control, and mad with the knowledge that they were free, about ten thousand of these pilgrims began to plunder the neighbouring country, and finally made their way under the very walls of Nicæa, where the Turks were encamped. Here, under the daring leadership of one Reinaldo, they actually took a fortress, and, when the Turkish Sultan advanced against them from Nicæa, left a good part of their army to defend it while the rest came face to face with the troops of Islam.

Needless to say, the pilgrims were hopelessly defeated; only their leaders and a handful of men escaped to the fortress, but even here there was no safety for them. The Sultan did not even trouble to besiege it. He merely starved them out until they were forced to yield. The end of the story is a dismal one, seeing to what end the pilgrims had pledged themselves. Offered the alternative of death or Islam, by far the greater number accepted the latter, and the few faithful were slain before their eyes.

A cruel trap was laid for that section of the army which had stayed behind with Walter the Penniless. The Turks, whose troops were now harassing the Christian camp, caused a rumour to be spread that Reinaldo and his men had taken possession of Nicæa. At once the camp rose like one man and demanded a share in the plunder. In vain Walter warned, entreated, threatened; heedless of his warning, the infatuated pilgrims rushed towards the city, unhindered, until they found themselves in the midst of a large plain before the walls. Then, all at once the troops of the Sultan David flung themselves upon them from every side. Helpless they fell, with Walter in their midst. About three thousand managed to escape, and fled back to Constantinople, the rest of that vast host either perished on the field or were brutally massacred afterwards by their conquerors.

Knowing nothing of the awful failure of their predecessors, a third army, led by a German priest named Gotschalk, advanced as far as Hungary. There the story almost repeats itself. The people of Hungary refused to let them pass through; and their king, panic-stricken at their appearance, captured them by a cruel trick. Calling them to his presence, he told them that his people only opposed them because they came in hostile fashion; but if they would lay down their arms, they should be protected during their passage through his country, and have their weapons restored on the frontier. This the unhappy pilgrims did, to be immediately massacred by the Hungarians.

Twice again we hear of the setting out of lawless troops, bent even more openly on plunder than their predecessors, and twice again we hear of the Danube running red with the blood of those slain by the hosts of Carloman of Hungary.

Nothing, of course, could have been hoped from such undisciplined hordes; but perhaps they served the purpose, at the cost of a quarter of a million lives, of warning the more thoughtful Crusaders of the dangers of the way, and, of the need of absolute control and able guidance.

And thus, "the chaff being winnowed with the fan out of God's store, the good grain began to appear."

CHAPTER VI

The Story of the Emperor Alexios and the First Crusade

Nought is more honourable to a knight
Nor battle doth become brave chivalry
Than to defend the feeble in their right
And wrong redress in such as wend awry
While those great Heroes glory got thereby.

SPENSER: *Faery Queene.*

In the August of 1096, the first great army of the Crusaders began to move towards the East, under the command of Godfrey of Boulogne, together with his brothers Eustace and Baldwin.

This Godfrey, leader of the Teuton host, is thus described by one of his own day: "He was of a beautiful countenance, tall of stature, agreeable in his discourse, of excellent morals, and at the same time so gentle that he seemed better fitted for the monk than for the knight. But when his enemies appeared before him, and the combat was at hand, his soul became filled with a mighty daring; like a lion, he feared not for his own person; and what shield, what buckler, could withstand the fall of his sword?"

Four other armies set out after him in due course, travelling by land to Constantinople; for, in those days, not even the stoutest general could face the horrors of a sea-voyage in the untrustworthy vessels of the Mediterranean shore.

Marching through Europe in perfect order, Godfrey's troops met their first check on the borders of Hungary. Here they not only found the track marked out by the bodies of those who had perished in the previous year, but a distinct air of hostility was seen in the attitude of the people. Knowing nothing of the actual facts, Godfrey cautiously arranged for a meeting with King Carloman.

Matters were explained on both sides and a mutual arrangement was made by which Godfrey's troops were allowed to pass through Hungary buying food as they went, while Baldwin, the brother of Godfrey, with his wife and children remained behind as hostages until the Crusaders should arrive at the further boundary—the River Save.

"So, day by day, in silence and peace, with equal measure and just sale, did the duke and his people pass through the realms of Hungary."

Once within the Emperor's domains, one would have thought the Crusaders on safe ground. But this was by no means the case. The second army of the Crusaders, which started almost at the same time as the first, was led by the brother of the French King, Hugh of Vermandois, a headstrong and self-willed prince. He chose, together with Robert of Normandy, son of the Conqueror, and some less important leaders, to make his own way through Italy in disorderly fashion; and after leaving in that pleasant land many of his followers with Duke Robert, he embarked at Bari for the East. A tempest cast him on the Austrian coast, which was under the Emperor's rule. Hugh at once despatched four and twenty knights dressed in golden armour to demand a fitting reception for himself and his followers; and was answered by the arrival of an armed escort, which led him as a prisoner before the Governor. There was some excuse for the conduct of Alexios, extraordinary as it seems; for, so far, the hordes of so-called Crusaders had brought such desolation and destruction upon his land that he had come to the conclusion that the Turks, at this time apparently inactive, were safer neighbours than the troops of Christendom. But Alexios was as wily as he was timid. After a short imprisonment, Hugh was brought to Constantinople and treated as the honoured guest of the Emperor—treated indeed so well that he fell a victim to his host's perfidious charm, did homage to him, and promised to persuade the other chieftains to follow his example.

This was the state of affairs when Godfrey of Boulogne appeared on the plains of Thrace, and hearing of the imprisonment of Count Hugh, he sent at once a peremptory message to demand his release. This demand met with absolute refusal, upon which Godfrey promptly gave orders to ravage the surrounding country.

Duke Godfrey marching through Hungary

Immediately alarmed, as usual, by the prospect of armed conflict, Alexios implored Godfrey to desist and to meet him in friendly conference at Constantinople. To this Godfrey agreed, and was met by Hugh himself outside the city walls. The latter sang the praises of the Emperor with enthusiasm, but Godfrey was still on his guard. A warning had reached him from some French merchants living in the city that treachery was meditated; and he therefore refused either to enter within the walls or to partake of the rich food which the Emperor sent to the camp.

Then Alexios vainly tried to persuade the Crusader to settle his army for the winter in the luxurious quarters of the Greek nobles across the Bosphorus, where they would act as a buffer between Constantinople and hostile forces from the East, at the same time removing themselves to a safe distance from the city.

This also Godfrey refused; and the alarm of the Emperor grew into panic when he realised that the army of another Crusader, Bohemond, his ancient enemy, who had already established a claim upon a large part of his Empire, was fast nearing his boundaries. It was absolutely necessary to make friends with Godfrey before the arrival of the dreaded Bohemond. As there seemed a possibility of the Crusaders, in their wrath at the refusal of supplies, attacking the city itself, a compact was made. Godfrey had no desire to use up his strength in fighting fellow-Christians, and readily accepted the Emperor's terms. The son of Alexios was sent as hostage to his camp, and the leaders, on their side, swore fealty to the Emperor for the time they were obliged to remain on his borders, and forthwith entered the city in peace and security.

But Alexios was still consumed with secret terror of the vast host which had swarmed into his land; and, on the pretext of an insufficient food supply, he managed to persuade Godfrey, after a brief sojourn, to transport his troops across the Bosphorus. With his usual craft, he then arranged that the vessels which had taken them over should immediately return.

Meantime the dreaded arrival of Bohemond, Prince of Tarentum, had actually taken place. A weak attempt was made to drive him back by force; but this was quickly overcome, and when Bohemond sent the prisoners taken in the conflict back to the

Emperor with an indignant and reproachful message, the wily Alexios promptly disowned all knowledge of the affair, professed the most affectionate regard for his ancient enemy, and sent him a pressing invitation to visit the capital city.

Now Bohemond was of a very different nature from the simple and upright Godfrey of Boulogne. He was an excellent leader, bold and skilful in warfare, but his character was warped by a mean, designing, and crafty spirit which entirely incapacitated him from playing a heroic part. When met by Godfrey in Constantinople and informed by him of the terms made with Alexios, he declared at first that nothing in heaven or on earth should induce him to swear fealty to his former foe. The Emperor ceased to press the matter, and merely treated him with more than ordinary magnificence of hospitality. Then, as though by chance, the Count was one day taken by an officer to a great room in the palace, crammed with costly jewels, ornaments of gold and silver, rich silks and brocades. The man's weak point had been observed too well. "What conquests might not be made if I possessed such a treasure!" cried Bohemond.

"It is your own!" replied the officer. The promise of an independent lordship near Antioch completed the bribe, and Count Bohemond was no longer to be feared.

Map of the Crusades

Of very different stuff was Raymond, Count of Toulouse, the first to volunteer but the last of the Crusading chiefs actually to set out for the East. He was now over fifty years of age, and, declaring that that was the last journey he should ever make, he determined to be well prepared. With the idea of choosing a route as yet untried by his predecessors, Raymond took his way through Lombardy into the desolate country of Dalmatia and Slavonia.

"It was already winter," says a writer of the time, "when Raymond's men were toiling over the barren mountains of Dalmatia, where for three weeks we saw neither beast nor bird. For almost forty days did we struggle on through mists so thick that we could actually feel them, and brush them aside with a motion of the hand." The weak, the sick, and the old suffered terribly from the attacks of the wild natives upon their rear; the bareness of the country gave no chance of even purchasing food, much less of foraging. It was with intense relief that they entered the Emperor's domains, "for here," writes one of the travellers, "we believed that we were in our own country; for we thought that Alexios and his followers were our brothers-in-arms."

In this belief the troops of Raymond found themselves mistaken, for they were harassed on all sides by the Emperor's soldiers. Alexios, as usual, disclaimed all responsibility, and begged the Count to hasten to Constantinople. There, to his disgust, the old warrior found that Godfrey, Bohemond, and the other leaders had all taken the oath of fealty, and were very anxious that he should follow their example. This Raymond emphatically refused to do. "Be it far from me," said he to Alexios, "that I should take any lord for this way save Christ only, for whose sake I have come hither. If thou art willing to take the cross also, and accompany us to Jerusalem, I and my men and all that I have will be at thy disposal."

Meantime came news to the Count that the army he had left when he accepted the call to Constantinople, had been attacked by the troops of the perfidious Emperor, whose aim, possibly, was to frighten Raymond into submission; but he had quite mistaken his man. Furious at this treachery, Raymond called upon his colleagues to join him in an attack upon the capital. But here he met with unexpected opposition. Bohemond, indeed, went so far as to threaten that if an open conflict took place, he would be found on the side of the Emperor, and even Godfrey urged most strongly that he should overlook everything rather than weaken their cause by fighting against fellow-Christians.

Strangely enough, though Raymond accepted unwillingly the advice of Godfrey, his upright character and vigorous simplicity seem to have won the respect and affection of the Emperor more than all the rest. It is true that Raymond refused steadfastly to pay him homage, "and for that reason," says the chronicler, "the Emperor gave him few gifts"; but we read in the record of the daughter of Alexios, who gives us a vivid account of this period, "One of the Crusaders, Count Raymond, Alexios loved in a special way, because of his wisdom, sincerity, and purity of life; and also because he knew that he preferred honour and truth above all things."

By this time such remnants of the army as had lingered in Italy under Robert of Normandy, together with all that was left of the rabble led by Peter the Hermit, had joined the main body of the Crusaders and were ready to advance upon the Turkish stronghold of Nicæa.

The full array of the armies of the First Crusade, before they were decimated by war and famine, must have constituted a truly overwhelming force. Their number must have been about six hundred thousand; in the words of the daughter of Alexios, "all Europe was loosened from its foundation and had hurled itself against Asia." The horsemen wore coats of mail, with pear-shaped shields, each with its own device, and carried a long spear and short sword or battle-axe. The foot-soldiers bore the cross-bow or long-bow, with sword, lance, and buckler. "They were covered," says a Saracen historian, "with thick strong pieces of cloth fastened together with rings, so as to resemble dense coats of mail."

Such was the appearance of the host which now marched upon the stronghold of Nicæa to begin a siege which is memorable for the light it throws upon the despicable character of the Emperor Alexios.

When the Crusaders first drew near to the city, says one of them, "the Turks rushed to war, exultingly dragging with them the ropes wherewith to bind us captive. But as many as descended from the hills remained in our hands; and our men, cutting off their heads, flung them into the city, a thing that wrought great terror among the Turks inside."

After this defeat the Sultan David deserted the city and hastened away to rouse his countrymen to give active help at this crisis; and the Crusaders, much encouraged, renewed the siege. The great obstacle to success was the fact that the city was protected on the west by a lake, which made it impossible to surround the walls. Aid was sought of Alexios, who sent boats from which skilful archers poured their arrows against the ramparts. It was evident that these must very shortly fall.

Knowing this to be the case, the Emperor sent a secret envoy to offer the Turks better terms than could be expected from the Crusaders, if they would give up the city to him.

Hence, just as the latter were preparing to make their last assault, they saw, with a disappointed fury that can be imagined, the Imperial flag floating from the citadel. The glory and the spoils of victory were both with Alexios, and though he tried to smooth the matter over by lavishing gifts upon the Crusaders, the feelings of the latter were truly expressed by Count Raymond when he said, "Alexios has paid the army in such wise, that, so long as ever he lives; the people will curse him and declare him a traitor."

CHAPTER VII

The Siege of Antioch

The faithful armies sang
"Hosanna to the Highest." ... Now storming fury rose
And clamour, arm on armour clashing brayed
Horrible discord.

MILTON: *Paradise Lost.*

The city of Antioch, capital of Syria, towards which the faces of
the Crusaders were now set, was one of the most famous and
beautiful cities of the East. Behind it lay the rugged ranges of
Lebanon; part of its wide girdle of walls and turrets was washed by
the river Orontes, towards which sloped gardens fragrant with
roses; and it was intersected by a spacious street adorned with
double' colonnades. But it was yet more famous for its associations
with St Peter, its first bishop, and for having been the birthplace of
St Chrysostom, "the golden-mouthed" teacher of Eastern
Christendom.

A few days after the march from Nicæa to Antioch had
commenced, the great army divided itself into two parts, one led
by Raymond, Baldwin, and Godfrey; the other by Bohemond,
Tancred, and Robert of Normandy. This division suited the plans
of the Sultan David, who, since the fall of Nicæa, had been
watching operations from the surrounding heights.

No sooner was Bohemond's army seen to halt for rest and
refreshment beside a river, than, with a terrific uproar, thousands
of Turks hurled themselves upon them from the heights above.
Hasty messages were sent to summon the other army, and
meantime the Crusaders fought with desperate valour.

"Even the women were a stay to us, for they carried water for our
warriors to drink, and ever did they strengthen the fighters."

The numbers of the foe were overwhelming, however, and only the courage and energy of the leaders prevented a panic-stricken flight. The tact of Robert of Normandy, who, at a critical moment, snatched off his helmet and cheered on his men in the thick of the fight, is said to have turned the scale of victory. Even then success seemed hopeless, but just as evening drew rapidly on, the second army came upon the scene. Seeing this, the Sultan fled, and many of his followers with him, but he left behind so rich a spoil of gold, jewels, silks, and other luxuries, that it was with difficulty the victors were induced to leave the booty and resume their march without too much encumbrance.

Such was the first pitched battle between the Crescent and the Cross, of which one of the combatants writes: "Had not the Lord been with us, and sent us speedily another army, not one of our men would have escaped."

And now the Crusaders were free to pass on to Antioch, though the march thither probably cost them more lives than did that battle of Dorylæum.

The heat of the desert wastes during the month of July left many prostrate by the wayside, never to rise again. Terrible thirst tormented them, and the sight of a welcome stream was the signal for such excesses of drinking that both men and horses died by hundreds.

It was almost impossible to obtain food, for the son of Sultan David had marched before the Crusading host, destroying all supplies and leaving the towns upon the track empty and famine-stricken.

At length the fertile district of Cilicia was reached, and relief was obtained from these woes. But here arose those unfortunate dissensions which were a lamentable feature both in this and later Crusades.

Robert of Normandy at Dorylæum

Robert of Normandy at Dorylæum

Meantime Tancred and Baldwin with a part of the army had pushed on to Tarsus. This city, the birthplace of St Paul, though held by a small band of Turks, was largely inhabited by Christians, who eagerly claimed Tancred as their protector and lord. Just as the Turks were about to surrender to him, the forces of Baldwin, who had been exploring elsewhere, appeared on the distant heights, and being mistaken by the Turks for their allies, encouraged them to delay giving up the city.

The arrival of the new-comer before the walls gave rise to a quarrel with Tancred, the heat of which was only intensified by the discovery that the unscrupulous Baldwin was busy intriguing with the inhabitants with the object of winning their allegiance.

In disgust, Tancred, the weaker but more upright of the two, left him to take possession of the city and marched to Messis. But thither, too, the grasping Baldwin followed, and the sight of his tents pitched beneath the walls was the signal for a conflict between the two hosts of Crusaders which reflects little credit on either side.

Finally, since reconciliation was impossible, Baldwin gladly accepted an invitation from the famous Armenian city of Edessa to take up its cause against the Turks. The prince adopted him as his son, and was ill rewarded by a rebellion of his people in favour of the new-comer, which soon cost their ruler his life. Thus, while the main army was pressing on to Antioch, Baldwin, married to an Armenian princess, was busy in establishing in Edessa the first Latin kingdom of the East.

On October 21st, 1097, the host of the Crusaders at length encamped around the walls of Antioch and made their preparations in anticipation of an early victory. The gates, however, were blocked by huge masses of rock from neighbouring quarries, and it seemed an easier task to break the walls than to force the gates.

But both proved to be impossible, even with the aid of a new instrument of war, a huge tower, the outcome of great toil and expense, which, full of troops, was wheeled against one of the gateways. This proved a failure before the showers of Turkish arrows, and was burnt to ashes as it stood.

Three months of fruitless effort passed, and the host of the Crusaders began to suffer from lack of food. They dared not venture far to look for it, for the Turks were always on the watch, and no man could with safety leave his post.

Finding, moreover, that the Crusaders generally got the worst of it when the Turks made a sally from the city, the native Christians of the country transferred the provisions they had been wont to bring to the former, to those from whom they now believed they would reap the greater advantage in the near future.

Then hope began to fail the besiegers, whose camp, owing to the heavy rain, had now become a fever-haunted swamp. One or two of the meaner-spirited leaders tried to get quietly away with their troops; even Peter the Hermit lost heart, and would have deserted the host had he not been forcibly turned back by Tancred.

Meantime the Seljukian Turks had been expelled by the Saracens from Jerusalem and Tyre, and the Caliph of the latter now sent envoys to the leaders of the Crusade, of whose evil condition he had been informed, to express his surprise that the Christians, while rightly warring against the fierce Seljuks, should desire to attack Jerusalem also. He promised, moreover, to extend his protection for a whole month to any peaceable pilgrims who should wish to visit the Holy City, on condition that the Crusaders would acknowledge his supremacy in Syria; and he warned them that if they refused his terms his whole power would forthwith be directed against them.

The Caliph's envoys expected to find the camp in sorry plight; but, to their surprise, they were entertained in lordly fashion, and found every sign of prosperity and plenty. They were sent back with an absolute refusal to relinquish the right of Christendom over the whole of Palestine, and quite in ignorance of the terrible straits in which the army really stood, in spite of its outward appearance of prosperity. It was true that when the enemy attacked them in the open, the Crusaders were more than able to hold their own; it was the hopeless inaction, the dread of disaffection in the camp, and the pangs of actual famine that were sapping the courage of the besiegers; and now the news that an immense army, led by the

Sultan of Persia, was coming to the relief of the city was the last and most crushing blow.

At this crisis, Bohemond, whose movements had for some time been full of mystery, assembled the leaders and asked for a solemn oath from them that the man who succeeded in taking the city should be its future ruler. Very unwillingly they gave their consent, upon which Bohemond revealed the fact that he had for some time past been in communication with an officer of the city guard, who was in the full confidence of the governor, and could obtain possession of Antioch whenever he wished.

So, on the 2nd of June 1098, nearly six months after the beginning of the siege, a little band of Crusaders quietly approached the gate of St George and gave their signal. A rope ladder was silently lowered from the top of the wall, up which Bohemond promptly sprang. But at the summit he found himself alone; for in their distrust of him, the rest had waited to see what would happen. The sight of his safe arrival gave them confidence, and about sixty swarmed up the ladder, which then broke. Those at the top, however, undeterred by their isolated position on the walls of a hostile city, found their way in the darkness to a gate, and broke it open. In rushed the invading army with their battle-cry of "Deus vult! Deus vult!" and the city, taken quite unawares, was soon in their hands.

The sun rose on the third day of June upon a city red with blood, the governor of which had paid with his head for his courage in holding out so long. Dawn also revealed the blood-red banner of Bohemond floating from the highest tower. Only the citadel, by a strange oversight on the conqueror's part, was still in the hands of a small body of Turks.

The news of the fall of Antioch gave rise to general alarm throughout the East. The followers of Sultan David, their former foe, joined with those of the Sultan of Persia against the Crusaders, and led by the famous general Kerboga, flung themselves against the walls of the city. Flushed with success, the victors had overlooked the fact that there was scarcely any food within the gates, and also they had allowed their means of access to the Mediterranean ports to be cut off. Within a few days the besiegers were the besieged and in far worse plight than before. Many, even of the nobles, were seized with panic, and letting themselves down by ropes from the walls, fled to the sea-coast. Even Stephen of Chârtres, son-in-law of William the Conqueror, who, through illness, had retired before the city fell, and who was now entreated to return with his troops to its aid, lost his nerve when he looked down from the hills upon the sea of tents that lay before the walls. Not only did he rapidly retreat, but meeting the Emperor Alexios marching with an army to aid the Crusaders, he actually prevailed upon the latter, not at all against his will, to retire from the hopeless conflict.

With foes outside the walls, and foes holding the citadel within, the unfortunate host of Crusaders was indeed in evil case.

"We who remained," writes one, "could not hold out against the arms of those within the castle, so we built a wall between ourselves and them, and watched it day and night."

Despair led to loss of nerve and discipline; many of the soldiers refused to bear arms or even leave their abodes, and had to be "burnt out" by the orders of Bohemond. The destruction of a great part of the city to which this inadvertently led, did not improve matters.

The situation was relieved at this apparently hopeless juncture in a most remarkable manner. Into the midst of the council at which the chiefs were hurriedly considering what could best be done to prevent further demoralisation, appeared a certain priest, Peter Barthelemy, chaplain to Raymond of Toulouse, who declared unto them a marvellous dream or vision. He had, he said, been carried in his sleep by St Andrew to the Church of St Peter within the city, and had been shown there the head of the lance which had pierced the sacred side of the Saviour. This, the saint had told him, if borne at the head of the army, was certain to bring them success.

Great was the power of religious faith in those days. Whether the story was true, or merely a device to drive out panic and awaken enthusiasm, matters not; the effect remains the same. Marching in solemn procession to the Church of St Peter, they made excavations at the spot indicated, at first with no success. Then as the dusk began to fall, Peter the priest himself descended barefooted and dressed only in a tunic, and after digging for some time, declared with a joyful shout that the sacred relic was discovered.

"At last," says the historian, "seeing that we were fatigued, the young man who had told us of the lance leapt into the pit, all ungirt as he was, without shoes, and in his shirt. He adjured us to call upon God to render us the lance for our comfort and our victory. At last the Lord, moved by such devotion, showed us the lance. And I, who have written these things, as soon as ever the blade appeared above ground, greeted it with a kiss, nor can I tell how great joy and exultation then filled the city."

Such was the effect of this discovery, that, in their certainty of victory, the Crusading chiefs forthwith sent a message to Kerboga, offering him a chance of withdrawal before he was utterly demolished. Peter the Hermit was the chosen ambassador, who, in spite of the courteous hospitality with which he was received, so disgusted the leaders of the host of Islam by his haughtiness and insolence, that no such peaceful arrangement could be entertained. "So much the better," said the rank and file, who were now as keen to fight as they had before been to escape. And so, very early on a perfect June morning, the army marched out through the rose-scented air in twelve battalions, according to the number of the twelve apostles, led by Bishop Adhemar with the Holy Lance held on high.

Some say that Kerboga was taken by surprise, others that he welcomed the opportunity, long hoped for, of drawing them into the open plain, and that he had planned to surround them from the rear, and cut them off from the city. However that may have been, a desperate struggle now began, which, from the overwhelming numbers of the foe, must in the ordinary course have gone against the Crusaders, weakened as they were by want of food. But it was the old story of the victory of mind over matter.

When Adhemar, deserted by Godfrey and Tancred, who had been summoned to the aid of Bohemond, hard pressed by David the Sultan, found himself surrounded by the dark face of the infidel, the sight of the Holy Lance moved his handful of followers to fight with such desperate valour, that for a moment the foe fell back. Raising his eyes to the encircling mountains, the Bishop saw, or thought he saw, three radiant figures riding upon milk-white horses to their aid.

"Behold, soldiers, the succour that God has provided for you!" he cried, and at once a shout went up from all parts that St George, St Theodore, and St Maurice had come to their help.

"Deus vult! Deus vult!" they cried, and Islam shrank before the extraordinary enthusiasm of their attack.

The story of the battle is a monument to religious faith, and illustrates in a wonderful way what miraculous deeds of valour can be wrought under its influence.

Ere long the Turks fled in confusion to the mountains, leaving the ground strewn with the bodies of the slain.

"But us the Lord multiplied," says he who tells the tale, "so that in battle we were more than they, and returning to the city with great joy, we praised and magnified God, who gave the victory to His people."

It is a pity that the sequel of the story fails to preserve this high level of enthusiasm and devotion. Had it been possible to march directly to Jerusalem, such might have been the case; but the burning heat of summer forbade such a course. Left idle in Antioch, the soldiers grew mutinous, and their leaders quarrelsome. Bohemond excited jealousy by his conquests of neighbouring cities. Hugh of Vermandois deserted with his troops and returned home. A pestilence, caused by the thousands of unburied bodies of the slain, fastened upon the Crusaders, and claimed amongst its victims the good Bishop Adhemar, the first to take up the Cross in the Holy War.

Not till January 1099 did the army march out towards the South, leaving Bohemond behind as Governor of Antioch.

It was upon this journey that Peter Barthelemy once more became prominent by reason of many new visions and dreams. But his master, Count Raymond, was unpopular at that time, and the occasion was seized by his opponents to accuse him indirectly of fraud in the matter of the Holy Lance. Whether this was true it is impossible to say; but it must be remembered that Peter himself never ceased to affirm his sincerity, and confidently offered to go through the terrible Ordeal by Fire in proof of the latter.

"Make me the biggest fire you can, and I will pass through the midst with the Lord's Lance in my hand. If it be the Lord's Lance may I pass through unharmed; if not, may I be burnt up."

A vast crowd of Crusaders gathered to witness the ordeal early on the morning of Good Friday. Peter, clad only in his tunic, passed fearlessly through the midst of two blazing piles of dead olive branches, a foot apart from one another. "God aid him!" cried a thousand throats, and when he emerged, apparently unhurt, a thousand hands were stretched out to feel his limbs and flesh. For the moment faith again seemed to have triumphed, and the followers of Raymond rejoiced. But presently it was seen that the unhappy priest was in terrible suffering, some say from burns, others from the too eager handling he had received from the crowd. He died a few days later, confident in his honesty to the last, and leaving those who had scoffed and those who had believed exactly in the same frame of mind.

Yet this much attacked and possibly deluded priest had done an important work; for, as far as we can see, the Holy War would have come to an abrupt end during the latter part of that remarkable siege of Antioch, had it not been for the almost miraculous spirit of zeal and devotion aroused by his alleged discovery.

CHAPTER VIII

The Holy City is won

Jerusalem, through the clear atmosphere, rising out of the deep umbrageous valleys which surround it, is reflected in a fiery splendour in the morning sunlight. FARRAR: *Life of Christ.*

Our feet shall stand within thy gates, O Jerusalem!

PSALM cxxii.

It was with high hearts that the remnant of the crusading host, now much reduced, took the road to the Holy City, the end of all their endeavours. With little difficulty they made their way along the smiling plain of the River Orontes, and then keeping close to the coast line between the mountains of Libanus and the sea, passed through the famous cities of Tyre, Sidon, and Joppa.

From the last of these they turned inland, and taking possession of the little town of Ramleh, supposed to be the burial place of St George, the patron saint of England, the leaders held a council to consider their next movements.

Those who cared most for the mere worldly success of the undertaking were now strongly of opinion that they should leave Jerusalem untouched for the present, and attack the true centres of the power of Islam, Babylon and Alexandria. Others reminded these men of the real object of the Crusades, and asked scoffingly how they hoped to seize great and populous cities if they could not first capture the little town of Jerusalem. The worldly-minded gave way, but consoled themselves by capturing villages and farms on the route of march. The rest, more serious minded, "set their faces steadfastly to go towards Jerusalem." "And those to whom the Lord's command was dearer than lust of gain, advanced with naked feet, sighing heavily for the disdain that the others showed for the Lord's command."

Whilst resting at Emmaus at nightfall of June 6, 1099, a little band of Christians living at Bethlehem crept into the camp and told the leaders a doleful story of the cruelty and oppression of Islam. The information that the birthplace of the Lord was near at hand quickened every pulse. Sleep was forgotten, and a hurried march begun which brought them in a few hours to the top of Mount Mizpeh, whence, with swelling hearts, they watched the sun rise upon the sacred walls of the Holy City.

"Jerusalem! Jerusalem!"

The cry, restrained and reverent, filled the morning air, as the great host fell prostrate and kissed the hallowed soil.

By its natural position the city was exceedingly difficult to take by assault, for it stood upon a rocky plateau, guarded by the two steep valleys of Kedron and Hinnon.

It was, moreover, defended by about forty thousand picked Saracen warriors—a band equal in number to that of the besiegers, but possessing far greater advantages as to position and supplies.

With the utmost confidence, however, the Crusaders took up their posts. Robert of Normandy being stationed on the north, Godfrey of Bouillon and Tancred on the west, while Count Raymond advanced to Mount Sion on the south.

It was clear from the first assault that they had undertaken no light task, and meantime the usual horrors of famine and thirst made their appearance in the camp. There was little shade in that region; the groves around had been cut down to provide wood for the "machines of war," and the chief water supply—a spring which bubbled up every other day—was soon choked by the corpses of men and beasts who had trodden one another down in the wild attempt to obtain drink.

The springs further off had all been poisoned by the Saracens, and when the supplies of fruit began to fail, it seemed as though the army would never possess the strength to attack the city again.

A still worse calamity was the quarrelling which now broke out again among the leaders. Tancred was bitterly censured for having set up his banner over the Church of the Nativity at Bethlehem, Raymond for having taken to himself the post of honour on the sacred Mount of Sion. The rank and file, following the example of their chiefs, gave themselves over to laxity, disobedience, and personal feuds.

Once again it was necessary to invigorate the faith of the Crusaders, and accordingly Peter the Hermit declared that the dead Adhemar had appeared to him with words of severe rebuke for the sins of the camp, and the promise that the city should fall if the army would march barefoot round it for the space of nine days. A council was summoned, at which the noble Tancred was the first to make up a long-standing quarrel with Count Raymond; a feeling of good-will and reconciliation was spread abroad; and it was determined to make a fresh attempt in a spirit of more fervid religious zeal.

On the 12th of July 1099, while the Saracens were setting up crucifixes upon the ramparts, and insulting their Christian foes by spitting and throwing mud upon them, a solemn procession, fully armed, singing psalms and litanies, made its way around the walls; and a sermon preached from the Mount of Olives by Arnulf, the future Bishop of Jerusalem, roused even the most despondent to do his best for the cause of God.

On the next two days, Wednesday and Thursday, assaults were made, but without much success. On the Friday the Crusaders, having been reminded that it was the day of the Lord's Passion and Death, came to the work with new vigour, "even the women and the children," writes the historian, "were eager to do their part on that field."

But when Count Raymond fought on the south of the city it seemed as though success was hopeless. His wooden tower, which protected the archers, was burnt by the throwing of flaming oil from the walls, and his men were driven into utter confusion. Suddenly, when retreat seemed inevitable, a marvellous portent was seen. On the Mount of Olives, on the further side of the city, appeared a knight in glittering armour, waving a flaming sword over Jerusalem. The rumour quickly spread that it was St George come to the aid of the Crusaders. "Deus vult! Deus vult!" they shouted, and in the vigour of their assault the outer wall was won.

The explanation of the occurrence was soon clear. At the further side of the city the stone-slingers of Godfrey of Boulogne had at length driven the Saracens from the ramparts. Seizing and lowering the drawbridge, and scrambling up the walls by scaling ladders, the Teuton host, headed by Bernard of St Valery, leapt upon the battlements. A certain unknown knight waved his sword in signal of victory from the top of Mount Olives, and this had been the sign which put new heart into Count Raymond's men.

At the very hour at which their Saviour breathed His dying words upon the Cross, the red-cross standard was first seen to float over the walls of the Holy City.

From the horrors of bloodshed that followed the capture of Jerusalem we can but turn away in disgust.

"Such a slaughter of pagan folk had never been seen or heard of; none know their number save God alone."

This wanton cruelty can indeed only be excused when we remember that it was the firm belief of those days that "whosoever killeth an infidel doeth God service."

After that scene of slaughter and violence the leaders of the Crusaders walked, bareheaded and barefooted, dressed in long white mantles marked with the red cross, to the Church of the Holy Sepulchre to offer thanks for their success. Amongst them stood Peter the Hermit, the real moving spirit of the Crusade, in spite of his mistaken zeal as a leader of men.

It is said that many of the Christian inhabitants of the city recognised him as the unknown pilgrim who had promised to rouse on their behalf the nations of the west, and they clung to his raiment with tears of gratitude. It is the last glimpse we have of that enthusiastic personality, and we may be content to leave him there, at the moment when his great aim had been accomplished.

The Storming of Jerusalem

A week later a meeting of the chieftains was called to elect a king of Jerusalem. None were eager to obtain a post of honour so difficult to maintain, and most were anxious to return to their own dominions. The crown was first offered to Robert of Normandy, who, "impelled by sloth or fear, refused it, and so aspersed his nobility with an indelible stain." So writes an English chronicler of his day, but it must be said in Robert's defence that, even as it was, he had tarried too long to make good his claim to the kingdom of England against his grasping brother Henry, and that his fair dukedom of Normandy stood in immediate peril from the same cause.

Finally, by universal consent, the crown fell to the lot of Godfrey of Boulogne, in many respects the noblest Crusader of them all. But he, with characteristic modesty, refused to wear a crown of gold in the place where his Lord had worn a crown of thorns, and so he was known only by the title of the Defender of the Holy Sepulchre. Some say that Count Raymond had previously been offered the position of king, and had refused to take it, hoping possibly that he might obtain the honour without the full responsibility. However this might be, we find him, on Godfrey's acceptance, sulkily retiring to the Tower of David, which stronghold had been seized from the Saracens by his men. At first he refused to give it up, and when forced to do so, declared with childish fury that he would go home at once.

Suddenly the intelligence that a vast army of Egyptians had gathered at Ascalon recalled men from such foolish bickerings, and united them once more for a time against the common foe. Although outnumbered by ten to one, the Crusaders were again victorious, for the enemy, according to the account of an eye-witness, seemed paralysed at the very sight of the Christians, "not daring to rise up against us." But this victory only served to fan the flame of the constant feud between Godfrey and Raymond. The latter had calmly accepted the allegiance of the people of Ascalon on his own responsibility. Godfrey naturally claimed the city as part of the kingdom of Jerusalem. Rumour accuses Raymond of having given back the town to the Egyptians rather than let it pass into the hands of Godfrey. He was scarcely pacified with the governorship of Laodicea, which was handed over to him when the other chieftains returned to Europe. Of those who had so gallantly turned their faces towards the East, Godfrey and Tancred remained in Jerusalem, Bohemond was ruler of Antioch, Baldwin of Edessa, Raymond of Laodicea.

The reign of Godfrey, first King of Jerusalem in all but name, lasted for barely one year. Gentlest of all the Crusaders, save where the "infidels" were concerned, and noblest of the knights of the chivalry of his age, he lived long enough to win the respect, if not the affection, of even the Moslem population of his kingdom, and to settle the latter upon a system scarcely differing from that of a feudal over-lordship in France or England.

His end came after an expedition undertaken to aid Tancred further up the coast. As he returned, he ate some fruit at Jaffa sent him by the Saracen ruler of Cæsarea. Immediately afterwards he was seized by sickness, and a rumour went round that the fruit had been poisoned. His one anxiety was now to return to the Holy City he had loved, and for which he had fought so well; and there he breathed his last in the July of 1100, and was laid to rest in the Church of the Holy Sepulchre.

In spite of all the intrigues of the partisans of Bohemond, the ambitious ruler of Antioch, the followers of the late king would have none but Baldwin, his brother, as his successor. The latter, therefore, was brought from Edessa, and became the first king, in name as well as in deed, of the Latin Kingdom of Jerusalem.

Let us now glance for a moment at the fate of some of those whose fortunes we have so far followed.

You will remember that among those who turned recreant before the siege of Antioch was Stephen of Blois, son-in-law of the Conqueror. When he returned to his wife Adela, she, with the blood of her father hot in her veins, bade him return and fulfil his oath. About the same time that he again turned his face to the East, a crowd of unruly Lombards, more eager for mere adventure than for the cause of God, set out for the Holy Land, and after a riotous sojourn at Constantinople, crossed the Bosphorus. There they were joined by Count Stephen, who begged the Emperor Alexios to furnish them with a guide to Jerusalem. The latter at once offered them Count Raymond, of stormy memory, who was staying at

Constantinople at the time. With him came the news that Bohemond of Antioch, over confident, had fallen into an ambush whilst on a foraging expedition, and was a prisoner in the hands of the Saracens.

Association with Raymond for however brief a period most assuredly resulted in a quarrel, and consequently there was a sharp difference of opinion as to the most advantageous route.

The Lombards would go across Asia Minor, rescue Bohemond, and possibly attack Bagdad, the centre of Moslem rule; whilst Count Stephen wished to follow the original road by way of Antioch.

Raymond elected to side with the latter, and together they set off upon a journey in which they were harassed hour by hour by their foes. The Lombards left without a guide, decided to follow in the rear, and had decidedly the worst of it, many of them being cut down by the Turks, who lay in ambush along the road. An engagement with the latter went against the Christians, a panic ensued, and, in the midst of the confusion, Raymond and his men rode off, and returned by sea to Constantinople, leaving his companions to their fate. With the utmost difficulty the remnant of the followers of the unfortunate Stephen made their way in the same direction.

After the usual recriminations were over, Count Raymond found himself next involved with Duke William of Aquitaine, who, with a great rabble of followers, had been stirred up by the news of the taking of Jerusalem, to seek high adventure in that quarter for himself. Other smaller expeditions followed, and setting off from Constantinople, fell straight into the hands of the Turks, who beset the track to the Holy Land. Of all these so-called Crusaders, barely one thousand survived to reach Antioch in the spring of 1102, and to make their way to Jerusalem.

Meantime Count Bohemond, having escaped from his two years' captivity, had not only resumed his position at Antioch, but had seized upon Raymond's territory of Laodicea as well. He was now the open and declared foe of Alexios of Constantinople, who had done his best to get the count into his hands by paying a huge ransom—a ransom which Bohemond himself had outbidden, and so won his freedom. Leaving Tancred to rule for him in Antioch, Bohemond now sailed to France, married the daughter of Philip I., with whose assistance he invaded the territory of the Emperor with a large army. Alexios, as usual, gave in and bribed him into a pretence of alliance, but a year later, when Bohemond had returned to Italy to gather fresh forces, death put an end to his fiery hopes and ambitions.

Meanwhile, when Bohemond on his escape was once more ruler of Antioch, Raymond, driven from Laodicea, had, as we have seen, joined the so-called "Aquitainian Crusade" for a time, and then set himself to win new territory by besieging the town of Tripoli. It is much to his credit that though, as his historian puts it, "he might have lived in abundance in his own land," he never ceased to fight while there was land to be won for Christendom. It is difficult, however, to avoid the suspicion that he was largely influenced by desire to serve his own personal ambitious ends. With but three hundred companions, Raymond attempted to carry on the siege of Tripoli; and there, an old and worn-out man, he died by the shores on which he had fought for the past six years.

The unfortunate Stephen of Blois had, meanwhile, wiped off the stain of desertion by his death in battle on the side of King Baldwin, against the Saracens; and Tancred, after holding Antioch for three years subsequent to the death of Bohemond, as regent for his little son, died of a wound received in a conflict with the Moslem foe.

Thus, by the year 1112, the only survivor in the East of that gallant band of crusading chieftains was Baldwin, brother of Godfrey, now King of Jerusalem.

In his reign were firmly established those great Orders of Knighthood, the Knights Templars and the Hospitallers, and the whole "Kingdom of Jerusalem" was settled upon a stronger basis—a strength, however, which was more apparent than real. Baldwin was a wise and skilful ruler, showing little of that mean and treacherous spirit which had distinguished his earlier career. He died in 1118, after a reign of seventeen years.

CHAPTER IX

The Story of Bernard of Clairvaux
and the Second Crusade

The rhythm of their feet,
The ineffable low beat
Of the vast throngs pacing slowly,
Floats on the sea of Time
Like a musical low chime
From a far Isle, mystic, holy.

L. MORRIS, *Marching.*

The First Crusade, with all its errors and shortcomings, may yet be counted as a success so far as the rescuing of Jerusalem from infidel hands was concerned.

The Second Crusade is one of the great failures of history. Yet the movement is associated with the name of one of the most notable characters of his age, the monk Bernard of Clairvaux. Just as in the First Crusade, the uneducated hermit, Peter, had appealed to the popular feeling of Europe, and had stirred up the poor and ignorant to do their best for the cause of God, so St Bernard, himself the son of a noble house, made his appeal first to the wealthy, to the crowned heads of Europe and the flower of their knighthood, and afterwards, by his zeal, his self-denying life, and his religious faith, to all those amongst whom he had earned the reputation of a saint.

During the years in which Bernard, as Abbot of Clairvaux, was devoting his energies to raising the standard of monastic life, affairs in the East had taken a distinct turn for the worse. The Saracens had grown stronger as the Christians grew more slack and careless. Baldwin III., a boy of thirteen, had come to the throne of Jerusalem two years before the first preaching of the Second Crusade, and held the reins of government with a weak and nerveless hand. A year after his accession, the kingdom of Edessa, the first to be established by Western Christendom in the East, had fallen into the clutches of the dreaded Sultan Zeuzhi.

The loss of Edessa sounded a trumpet note of alarm to the West. The hard-won success of the First Crusade was evidently trembling in the balance. Something must be done to establish and settle Christian dominion of the Holy Land upon a much firmer basis.

There were other motives at work as well. France, torn by the constant quarrels between its feudal lords, who only united with one another in order to defy their sovereign, could not be pacified save by some pressing call to arms outside. But the immediate cause that led the young French king Louis to take up the Cross was the feeling aroused throughout the religious world of the West by one desperate deed.

He was attacking the rebel town of Vitry, which cost him so much trouble to quell, that, in revenge, he not only destroyed the city, but set fire to a great church in which over a thousand people had taken refuge. The cries of the victims and the reproaches of his subjects combined to rouse the conscience of the king, who vowed to go on a pilgrimage to Jerusalem as a penance for his crime.

It was the Easter of 1146. On the top of the hill that overshadows the town of Vézelay, a wooden tower had been hastily raised, with a high platform in front, on which sat the beautiful proud Queen Eleanor amidst a bevy of her ladies, and the young king with the great cross upon his tunic. Suddenly there appeared in the midst of the gallant throng a thin pale-faced monk, eager and bright-eyed, followed by three bishops of the Church. Presently a vast crowd, stretching far away to the edge of the plain below the hill, was hanging breathlessly upon the words of the famous Abbot of Clairvaux, as, quietly at first, and then with the most eloquent persuasion, be bade them go forth to drive the unbeliever from the Holy Land.

A roar of enthusiasm arose from the multitude before his words were done.

"Crosses! Crosses!" cried the people; and when Bernard had flung to them those which lay in a great heap by his side, he tore up his own long robe to make them more.

The vast multitude dispersed, with the solemn pledge of Louis of France that, after one year of preparation, the Second Crusade should march towards the East.

But Bernard's aim was not yet accomplished. Conrad of Germany, whose possessions in that land were threatened on every side, held back from the Holy War. The monk followed him from place to place, persuading and threatening him in vain.

At length Conrad promised to give a definite answer on a certain day, and on that occasion, when the Emperor came to Mass, Bernard preached a sermon in which he described the Day of Judgment. There Conrad was depicted trembling before the judgment-seat as he was called to account for his great riches and power. "How have I, thy Lord, failed in aught of My duty towards *thee*, O man?" asks his Master. In the breathless pause that followed, the Emperor arose and cried aloud with tears, "No longer will I be ungrateful. I will serve Christ and take up His Cross whenever He shall call me!"

"Praise be to God!" shouted the assembled congregation, rising to their feet, and before the service was ended, Bernard had marked the King with the Cross, fastening upon his breast the sacred emblem torn from a banner from the high altar.

In the wave of enthusiasm that now swept over France and Germany as St Bernard went from town to town, preaching and exhorting, the women did not stand aloof. Queen Eleanor herself prepared to accompany her husband, Louis, and with her went a crowd of fair dames from France. With Conrad, too, marched a troop of women, bearing shields and swords, led by one known as the "golden-footed dame."

The German army started first and, save for floods by which some were drowned, and lack of discipline which ruined more, reached Constantinople in comparative safety. But here the behaviour of the drunken German soldiers, who wantonly destroyed the beautiful pleasure gardens of the city, and showed themselves utterly untrustworthy, created serious ill-feeling between Conrad and the Greek Emperor Manuel. The latter succeeded in inducing Conrad to transfer his army across the Bosphorus, on the promise that he would provide them with guides through Asia Minor; but he had meantime determined secretly to betray the armies of the West at the earliest opportunity.

The guides supplied by him were in the pay of the Turkish Sultan of that region, and after leading the unhappy men by dangerous roads and in wrong directions, finally brought them to a barren plain, without food or water, bordered by hills amongst which lurked thousands of the enemy. The guides then fled in the darkness, leaving the army to cope with an enemy whose sudden attacks and equally sudden disappearances among the rocky hills gave the Crusaders little chance of effective retaliation. Wounded and dispirited, the unfortunate Conrad at length turned back to Nicæa, his starting-place in Asia Minor, taking with him barely one-tenth of the army which had started from Germany.

Meantime, the treacherous Manuel had taken measures beforehand with regard to Louis. When the French armies reached his territory they found every city closed against them. Even when provisions might be bought, they were let down from the walls in baskets by the Greeks. This unfriendly spirit was not disregarded by the French nobles and clergy, some of whom urged their king to make war upon an Emperor whose cities were not invulnerable, and who was said to be in league with the Turks.

This, however, Louis steadfastly refused, and trusted that his well-disciplined army would win the favour of the Emperor—a favour that the Germans had certainly not deserved.

It seemed, indeed, as though this might happen, for when they drew near the city, a fine procession came forth to meet the King, and to conduct him with honour to the presence of the Emperor.

Before long "the two princes became as brothers." Manuel himself displayed to Louis the magnificent buildings of his city, and described to him the victorious march which Conrad, as he said, with his assistance, had made through Asia Minor. He offered the same aid in the way of guides to Louis, if he and his barons would pay the customary homage.

With high hearts the French started for Nicæa, but they had not long encamped in that place when some ragged and blood-stained fugitives brought the news of the disaster to Conrad's troops. At once Louis hastened to meet his brother sovereign; "weeping, they fell upon each other's neck," and agreed henceforth to keep together and to aid one another.

In dread of fresh attacks and more treachery, they turned from the beaten track, and passing along the coast, came at length to Ephesus. There a message reached them from Manuel, possibly repentant of his former treachery, to the effect that their further way was blocked by a huge army of Turks. Conrad, weak with wounds, then determined to return for awhile to Constantinople, but, acting on his advice, Louis, after staying to rest his troops and to let them spend their Christmas in a fertile valley hard by, moved on over the frozen hills to the River Meander, the opposite bank of which was lined with Turks. For awhile both armies marched along the banks of the river in parallel lines; then Louis discovered a ford, and thereupon made good his passage and inflicted a great defeat upon the foe.

But a terrible obstacle now faced them some miles beyond Laodicea; they found the way shut in by a steep range of hills "whose summit appeared to touch the heavens, whilst the torrent at its base seemed to descend to hell."

Sent forward to secure the pass, Geoffrey de Rancogne struggled to the top, but instead of taking possession of it, descended the further slope, and, oblivious of the fact that the heights were thronged with Turks, bade his men pitch their tents there. The main army, thinking all was well, followed them to the summit of the narrow pass, where a tremendous precipice skirted the track. Down rushed the foe upon them, hurling them into the yawning depths. A large number of the Crusaders, pilgrims, who were quite unarmed, blocked the way when Geoffrey strove to return to the rescue; thousands of these were massacred, and Louis himself only just managed to save his life by scrambling up to a high rock, from whence his well-made armour defied the arrows of his assailants.

For a while they sought to drive him from his position, but, not realising that he was the leader of the expedition, left him at nightfall to his fate.

This awful disaster nearly ended the Second Crusade there and then. Rage against Geoffrey de Rancogne for his error, and dismay at the slaughter of their fellow-soldiers, put an end to discipline for the time. It was only with the utmost difficulty that Louis was able to conduct a remnant of the army to the post of Attaleia; the rest had perished either by famine or by the constant attacks of the Turks upon their line of march.

At the coast it was hoped that the troops might be taken to Antioch by sea, and an attempt was made to arrange this with the Greeks who held the fort. They, however, demanded an impossible sum for the three days' voyage, and it was decided that the main army must go by land, in charge of Greek guides, while Louis and his barons crossed by sea. First, however, the King bargained to pay a large sum if the Greeks would receive into the city, and care for the large number of sick and infirm pilgrims; and this was readily promised. There was no reliance to be placed, however, upon the treacherous Greeks. Scarcely had the king's ship set sail than they betrayed the whole band of sick pilgrims into the hands of the Turks, and soon afterwards led the army also into the midst of the hordes of the infidel. The helpless misery of the victims touched the hearts even of the Turks, who pitied them and gave them food, "and therefore," says the historian, "many of the Christians forsook their own religion and went over to the Turks. O kindness more cruel than Greek treachery! For, giving bread, they stole the true faith.... God may indeed pardon the German Emperor, through whose advice we met with such misfortunes, but shall He pardon the Greeks, whose cruel craft slew so many in either army?"

Thus, by this twofold act of treachery, the Greeks, the representatives of Eastern Christianity, practically put an end to the Second Crusade. It was no triumphal entry that Louis of France made when, on reaching Jerusalem, he passed through the streets behind priests and bishops, who sang, "Blessed is he that cometh in the name of the Lord." He had come empty-handed, for the bones of his troops were scattered on the hills and plains of Asia Minor.

King Louis surrounded by the Turks 115

King Louis surrounded by the Turks

At Jerusalem Louis found that Conrad, travelling from Constantinople by water, had preceded him with a fairly numerous following. Feeling that something must be done towards fulfilling the aim with which they had set out, the two sovereigns joined with the young king, Baldwin of Jerusalem, in an attempt to besiege Damascus, still one of the most important cities of the Holy Land.

To this siege came the famous Knights of the Hospital and the Temple, and the combined troops fought with such success that the fall of the city seemed certain. Moreover, since they were attacking it from a quarter rich in orchards and springs, they had no fear of the ever-dreaded famine that had wrought such havoc in the First Crusade.

Then once again discord brought disaster. Heated discussions arose as to who should rule Damascus when it was taken, and the suggestion that it should be given to the Count of Flanders at once gave offence to the "barons of Palestine,"—those who had inherited the possessions of the First Crusaders. They actually began to enter into negotiations with the citizens of Damascus, and, playing the part of traitors, persuaded Louis, Conrad, and Baldwin that they would find the walls weakest at the farther side of the city. Falling into the trap, the three kings moved their camp, and soon found themselves cut off from all supplies of food and drink, and faced by hopelessly strong fortifications. So they gave up in despair. Conrad, in deep disgust, returned to Europe at once; Louis, after a short stay at Jerusalem, returned to France by sea, with a few wretched followers, in place of the gallant army that had marched forth barely a year before.

The utter failure of the Second Crusade—a failure which left countless homes in Western Europe empty and desolate—struck a heavy blow at the authority and popularity of Bernard of Clairvaux. He himself was not slow to point out the cause.

"We have fallen on evil days," says he, "in which the Lord, provoked by our sins, has judged the world, with justice indeed, but not with His wonted mercy. The sons of the Church have been overthrown in the desert, slain with the sword or destroyed by famine," and he goes on to say that this is due to allowing thieves and murderers to take part in an attempt which only the faithful and holy soul should be found worthy to make.

The chief result of the Crusade, as far as the Holy War itself was concerned, was to weaken the position of the Christians in that region; for as Fuller quaintly remarks, "The Turks, seeing one citie both bear the brunt and batter the strength of both armies, began to conceive that their own fear was their greatest enemy; and those swords of these new pilgrimes which they dreaded in the sheath, they slighted when they saw them drawn, and they shook off the awe which had formerly possessed them of the strength of the Western Emperor."

CHAPTER X

The Loss of Jerusalem

All Europe streaming to the mystic East:
Now on their sun-smit ranks
The dusky squadrons close in vulture-feast.

PALGRAVE: *Visions of England.*

Most famous of the Sons of Islam who fought against Christendom is Saladin, the Saracen general who made himself master of Egypt in the days of Amalric, King of Jerusalem, and who was destined in the near future to be the conqueror of the Holy City.

The time was ripe for such a conquest, for the little kingdom was torn by the jealousy and strife of two deadly rivals, Raymond of Tripoli and Guy of Lusignan.

The former was for living at peace with the Saracens, at least until the coming of a new Crusade should drive the infidel from the borders of the land. The latter, moved by causes far other than religious enthusiasm, was eager to fight at once, hoping thus to obtain the upper hand over his wretched young brother-in-law, Baldwin, the leper king. With him was Reginald of Châtillon, who had spent long years in Saracen dungeons, and was furiously eager for revenge.

The quarrel between Raymond and Guy and their adherents led directly to the Fall of Jerusalem, but in the meantime the details are full of romantic interest.

A certain Gerard, a knight of France, who had come to the Holy Land merely to make his fortune, desired to marry the Lady of Botron, a rich ward of Raymond of Tripoli. But Raymond, as was frequently the case in those feudal days, had his own profit to make by the marriage. He scornfully rejected Gerard, and gave the lady to a wealthy Italian merchant, who was glad to pay for his wife her weight in gold.

In great wrath, Gerard left Tripoli, joined the Knights Templars, and in due course became Grand Master of the Order, and awaited his chance for revenge. This came in 1186, when both the leper and his little son were dead, and Raymond was known to be desirous of occupying the vacant throne.

Hurriedly summoning Sibylla, wife of Guy of Lusignan, and sister of the leper king, to Jerusalem, Gerard and Reginald of Châtillon caused the gates to be shut and the walls guarded, so that none might come in or out. But amongst those inside was a spy sent by the watchful Raymond, who managed to get into the Church of the Holy Sepulchre, where he saw Sibylla sitting with two crowns before her. One of these was handed to her by the Patriarch of Jerusalem, who said, "Lady, you have been proclaimed queen, but since you are a woman, it is good that you have a man to help you in your rule. Take the crown you see before you and give it to him who can best help you to govern your realm."

Then Sibylla beckoned to her husband, Guy, and placing the crown upon his head as he knelt before her, said, "Sire, take this, for I know not where I could bestow it better."

Then was Gerard, Grand Master of the Templars, heard to murmur, "This crown is well worth the marriage of Botron."

Thus did Guy de Lusignan become King of Jerusalem, while Raymond of Tripoli, checkmated for the time, could only refuse him his allegiance and retire in sullen fury to his own city of Tiberias. Rumour indeed whispered that he was on no unfriendly terms with Saladin himself. But it was probably foresight as well as a sense of justice which roused him to deep wrath when Reginald of Châtillon, in time of truce, attacked a wealthy caravan passing from Damascus to Egypt, and "dishonourably carried off the merchants as prisoners, together with all their baggage."

"The taking of this caravan," says the chronicler, "was the ruin of Jerusalem," for from that time dates the implacable hatred of Saladin for those who held the city.

Meantime, urged on by Gerard, the Grand Master, Guy of Lusignan, meanest and weakest of kings, sought to gratify his personal spite against his former rival by besieging Tiberias, and was only prevented by a warning that this might mean an open alliance between Saladin and Raymond against himself.

Raymond's patriotism, however, was greater than his desire for revenge. While absent from his own city with his troops, he heard that the Saracens had crossed the Jordan, and were advancing upon the Holy City. Hastening to Jerusalem, he at once put himself and his men at Guy's disposal in face of this pressing danger.

Meantime Saladin, probably in wrath at this action of one whom he had hoped to make his ally, began to besiege Tiberias; and a message arrived in Jerusalem from Raymond's wife, begging that an army might be sent to her aid. A council was hurriedly summoned to see what could be done to save the city; but Raymond, to the surprise of all, was strongly of the opinion that Tiberias should be left to its fate.

"Sire," said he, "I would give you good advice if you would only trust me." "Speak your mind and fear nothing," they replied, whereupon he counselled them not to send troops out of Jerusalem, even if this should mean the loss of his own fortress.

"If I lose wife, retainers and city," said he, "so be it; I will get them back when I can; but I had rather see my city overthrown than the whole land lost."

Though much astonished by such disinterested advice, the council agreed to follow it, and so dispersed.

But at dead of night there came secretly to the King the mischief-maker Gerard, bidding him "reject the counsel of this traitor count," and hinting that Raymond's advice had been merely to further his own ends. Guy de Lusignan was so much in the hands of the man who had made him king that he dared not refuse to listen to him, and at daybreak the order was given for the army to march out of Jerusalem in order to relieve Tiberias.

In the terrible battle of Tiberias that followed, the portents were all against the Crusaders.

"A fearful vision was seen by the King's chamberlain, who dreamed that an eagle flew past the Christian army bearing seven darts in its talons, and crying with a loud voice, "Woe to thee, Jerusalem."

On a mound outside Tiberias had been placed a portion of the True Cross, and round this the army of Guy, unable to enter the city, rallied again and again as they were dispersed by the followers of Saladin. But heat and thirst played as much havoc as did the enemy, and at close of day, the sacred relic itself, together with the King and Reginald of Châtillon, the truce-breaker, fell into the hands of the infidel.

It is said that Reginald's head was struck off in the presence of Saladin, and possibly by his hand, in revenge for his past perfidy. Guy was thrown into prison, and Raymond, who had made good his escape, died of grief at the loss of all that he had held most dear.

Within two months of this battle of Tiberias, Saladin was master of every important stronghold in the land, save only Tyre and Jerusalem, and these were closely besieged.

The Holy City was indeed in the most perilous condition, for there were now no soldiers within the walls, and no leader to look to in all the land, save only Balian of Ibelin, and he was at this time a fugitive, who had sought protection within the walls of Tyre.

Bereft of a leader, the city had well-nigh lost hope, when Balian, acting apparently in good faith, begged leave of Saladin to conduct his wife and family within the walls of Jerusalem, promising that he himself would stay there but one night, and then return to Tyre.

To this Saladin agreed; but when Balian was once inside the city, the inhabitants refused to let him leave it again.

The patriarch Heraclius, indeed, assured him that he could not keep his promise without committing grave sin, saying, "Great shame will it be to you and to your sons after you if you leave the Holy City in this perilous strait."

So Balian remained and did his best, with only two knights to aid him, and little enough of food to feed the multitudes who came in day by day from the country round, and set up their tents in the streets of the city.

"The priests and clerks," says Geoffrey de Vinsauf, "discharged the duties of soldiers and fought bravely for the Lord's House ... but the people, alike ignorant and timorous, flocked in numbers round the patriarch and the queen, bitterly complaining and earnestly entreating that they might make terms of peace with the Sultan as soon as possible."

Even when the city was given up on condition that Saladin would accept a ransom for the lives of the inhabitants, there came small consolation to the unhappy people. For some thousands of them could pay no ransom at all, and had nothing to hope for but the miseries of slavery.

When this fact was known, it called forth all that chivalry of the infidel chieftains upon which the chroniclers love to dwell.

Saphadim, the brother of Saladin, and his right hand during the siege, at once begged a thousand slaves as his share of the booty.

"For what purpose do you desire them?" asked Saladin.

"To do with them as I will," replied his brother, upon which the Sultan smiled and granted his request.

As he expected, the unhappy captives were at once given their freedom. Then the Patriarch and Balian, who had been treated with the utmost courtesy, each begged for seven hundred souls; and when those were granted, Saladin said, "My brother has given his alms; the bishop and Balian theirs. Now will I give mine also."

With that he granted freedom to all aged folk within the city, "and this was the alms that Saladin made."

Thus did Jerusalem fall once more into the hands of Islam, and the Crescent shone again over the Holy City, in which for eighty-eight years the Cross had reigned supreme.

CHAPTER XI

The Story of the Third Crusade

A goodly golden chain wherewith yfere
The virtues linked are in lovely wise
And noble minds of yore allyed were
In brave pursuit of chivalrous emprise.

SPENSER: *Faery Queene.*

The news of the fate of Jerusalem moved Western Europe to such horror and dismay as had never before been known. Everywhere signs of mourning were seen; a general fast was ordered, a fast which was kept to some extent, at least, by some pious souls, until the Holy City was recovered; and Pope Clement III. set himself to act the part of a St Bernard by stirring the hearts of princes to take up the Cross in a Third Crusade.

Of this Crusade it seemed at first as though the famous Emperor Frederick Barbarossa was to be the leader, though Philip of France and Henry II. of England were not long behind him in accepting the Cross.

In both France and England, too, the "Saladin-tax" became the custom—each man paying a tithe, or tenth part of his income, for the maintenance of the expedition. Everywhere the enthusiasm was so great, that it was only necessary for a preacher to announce the Crusade as his text to secure a vast and eager audience. It mattered nothing that his hearers did not even understand the language in which he spoke—all alike were stirred to do their part to win back what the First Crusaders, those heroes of romance, had fought for and won.

But Henry of England was too fully occupied with the treason of his sons in his old age to do more than make promises of help, and at his death, it was one of the latter, the famous Richard Lion-Heart, who became the leader of the English Crusade, and finally of the whole undertaking. The Emperor Frederick, however, would not wait for him, nor for the French king, but hurried off on his toilsome journey at an age when most men would be hoping for a period of fireside ease and rest before the last long journey of all.

As usual the promises of the Greek Emperor, Isaac, were not to be trusted, but the great army of Frederick Barbarossa struck such terror into the hearts of Greek and Turk alike, that he was able to move forward into Cilicia with little hindrance. But there, when bathing his heated limbs in a little river among the hills, that mighty Emperor, who had built up a famous Empire of the West, perished and "came to a pitiful end."

The German host lost heart without their leader; many died through famine, and of the remainder a small part reached Antioch and placed themselves under the command of its prince, the rest going on to Tripoli.

Meantime those two ill-assorted leaders, Richard of England and Philip of France, had started on their way to the East. It was clearly hopeless from the first that they would work together, for, while Richard was proud, passionate, and irritable to a degree, Philip was cold and crafty, and while Richard would eagerly make amends for an injury done, and as readily forgive one done to him, Philip prided himself on never overlooking an affront. It was the quarrel of these leaders, rather than the superiority of the armies of Islam, that made the Third Crusade, as far as the taking of Jerusalem was concerned, a complete failure.

They started, however, in apparent friendliness, and, with many pledges of devotion, travelled together by a new route by way of Marseilles. From thence Philip hurried on to Messina, in Sicily, but Richard's Crusaders had deviated into Portugal to give help against the Moors, and their impatient king set off alone in a small ship, coasting along the shores of Italy, until his fleet had caught him up, when he proceeded in great state to join Philip at Messina.

The Crusaders stayed in Sicily for six months, by no means in the character of friendly guests. Tancred, king of the island, had forced Joanna, the sister of Richard, to become his wife; and she appealed to her brother against him. The latter promptly took up her cause, but, with an eye to his own profit, offered to give her up if Tancred would grant him a chair and table of solid gold which formed part of her dowry. On Tancred's refusal, Richard at once attacked and took Messina, which was only recovered by Tancred on payment of forty thousand ounces of gold.

On the same March day that Philip at length sailed for the Holy Land, Richard was betrothed to the beautiful Berengaria of Navarre, and some ten days later set off with her and his sister for the same destination. But within two days a furious storm arose, which threw two of his ships upon the coast of Cyprus.

Says Richard of Devizes, "Almost all the men of both ships got away alive to land, many of whom the hostile Cypriote slew, some they took captive, some, taking refuge in a certain church, were besieged. The prince also of that island coming up, received for his share the gold and the arms; and he caused the shore to be guarded by all the armed force he could summon together, that he might not permit the fleet that followed to approach, lest the King should take again what had been thus stolen from him.... But God so willed that the cursed people should receive the reward of their evil deeds by the hand of one who would not spare. The third English ship, in which were the women, rode out at sea and watched all things, to report the misfortune to the king. A full report reached the King, who, obtaining no satisfaction from the lord of the island, came in arms to the port. The King leaped first from his galley and gave the first blow in the war, but before he could strike a second, he had three thousand of his followers with him striking away by his side.... The Cypriotes are vanquished, the city is taken, and the lord of the island is himself taken and brought to the King. He supplicates and obtains pardon; he offers homage to the King, and it is received; and he swears, though unasked, that henceforth he will hold the island of him as his liege lord, and will open all the castles of the land to him."

That same night, while Isaac of Cyprus was plotting how to get rid of his new-made bonds, Guy of Lusignan, the King of Jerusalem, who had been released by Saladin on condition that he went into exile, landed on the island to bring greeting to Richard. On the next day the faithless Isaac fled. "The kings pursue him, the one by land, the other by water, and he is besieged in the castle. Its walls are cast down by engines hurling huge stones; he, being overcome, promises to surrender if only he might not be put into iron fetters.

"The King consented to the prayers of the supplicant, and caused silver shackles to be made for him. The prince of the pirates being thus taken, the King traversed the whole island; and the whole land was subjected to him, just like England."

Before he left his new domain, Richard was married to Berengaria, his betrothed, and set off with her to the Holy Land, accompanied by Guy of Lusignan. Their destination was Acre, which, ever since Guy had been convinced by the clergy that his oath to Saladin was of no binding nature, had been besieged by him. When Richard arrived, this siege had already lasted nearly two years, and to a more cautious eye the cause of Guy of Lusignan would have appeared by no means hopeful. But there were other motives at work. Conrad of Tyre had flatly refused to admit Guy to his own city, now the only Christian stronghold in Palestine, on the plea that God had appointed him its ruler and that he meant to remain so. This laid the foundation of a fine feud between the two princes; and the fact that Philip of France had taken up the cause of Conrad was sufficient reason for Richard to ally himself with his rival.

"So," says Richard of Devizes, "King Richard came to the siege of Acre, and was welcomed by the besiegers with as great joy as if it had been Christ that had come again on earth to restore the kingdom of Israel. The king of the French had arrived at Acre first, and was very highly esteemed by the natives; but on Richard's arrival he became obscured and without consideration, just as the moon is wont to relinquish her lustre at the rising of the sun."

In further explanation of this, he tells us how a certain Henry, Count of Champagne, who had now used up the whole of his store of provision and money, came to his king, Philip of France, for relief. The latter, trying to take a mean advantage, offered him a large sum if he would give up his rights over Champagne; to which the Count replied, "I have done what I could and what I ought; now I shall do what I am compelled by necessity. I desired to fight for my king, but he would not accept of me unless I gave up what is mine own; I will go to him who will accept me, and who is more ready to give than to receive."

Richard received him with the utmost kindness and liberality, and his men, "at the report of so great a largess, took King Richard to be their general and lord; the Franks only who had followed their lord remained with their poor king of the French."

This did not endear Richard any the more to Philip, but for a while these private grudges were forgotten in the assault upon the walls of Tyre.

"The King of the English, unused to delay," says Richard of Devizes, "on the third day of his arrival at the siege, caused his wooden fortress, which he had called 'Mate Grifon,' where it was made in Sicily, to be built and set up; and before the dawn of the fourth day the machine stood erect by the walls of Acre, and from its height looked down upon the city lying beneath it, and there were thereon by sunrise archers casting missiles without intermission upon the Turks."

While the Kings of England and France were thus engaged, Conrad and Guy were once again at variance. With Philip's promise of support at his back, Conrad now returned to Tyre and took no further part in the siege. The sultry heat of the plain then struck down both Philip and Richard for awhile, but the recovery of the former led to an assault which showed the Saracens they had little hope of holding out, and Richard, determined not to be outdone, struggled back to the walls from his sick-bed, and struck them another heavy blow. Four days later a long procession of the citizens filed out from the gates, bearing a flag of truce and offering to surrender the city. Richard was for "letting the vanquished pay their heads for the ransom of their bodies," but Philip, more politic as well as more thrifty, held out for a ransom of two hundred pieces of gold, the restoration of the True Cross which Saladin had seized at the Battle of Tiberias, and the release of all Christian captives.

So the two years' siege came to an end, but not without a deed which blackens the name of Richard and Philip for all time.

Saladin had delayed to furnish the ransom or to give up the relics of the Cross; whereupon the King, who was in name the follower of Him who taught His people to love their enemies, had two thousand seven hundred prisoners led to the top of a hill from which all that went on could be seen in Saladin's camp; and there, at a given signal, all these innocent followers of Mohammed were cut down in cold blood. Almost at the same time, by the orders of Philip, nearly as many victims suffered on the walls of the city itself.

The taking of Acre was the signal for a violent quarrel between Richard, Philip, and Leopold, Duke of Austria.

Richard and Philip at the Siege of Acre

Richard and Philip at the Siege of Acre

Richard Devizes tells the story thus. "The Duke of Austria, who was also one of the ancient besiegers of Acre, followed the King of the English as though he would share in the possession of his portion; and because his standard was borne before him, he was thought to take to himself a part of the triumph. If not by the command, at least with the consent of the offended King, the duke's standard was cast down in the dirt, and to his reproach and ridicule, trampled under foot. The duke, though grievously enraged against the King, concealed his wrath for a time, and betook himself that night to his tent, which was set up again, and afterwards as soon as he could, returned, full of anger, to his own country."

Heedless of the fact that "this quarrel might drink blood another day," Richard next came into serious collision with Philip of France.

"A certain Conrad, Marquis of Montferrat, a smooth-faced man, had held Tyre, which he had seized on many years ago, to whom the King of the French sold all his captives alive, and promised the crown of the kingdom of Jerusalem, which was not yet conquered. But the King of the English withstood him, Philip, to the face."

"It is not proper," said he, "for a man of your reputation to bestow or promise what is not yet obtained; and further, if the course of your journey be Christ, when you have at length taken Jerusalem from the hand of the enemy, you will, without delay or condition, restore the kingdom to Guy, the lawful King of Jerusalem. For the rest, if you recollect, you did not obtain Acre alone, so that neither should that which is the property of two be dealt out by one hand."

"Oh, oh!" comments quaint Richard of Devizes, "how pure for a godly throat! The marquis, bereft of his blissful hope, returns to Tyre, and the King of the French, who had greatly desired to strengthen himself against his envied ally by means of the marquis, now fell off daily, and this added to the continual irritation of his mind—that even the scullion of the King of the English fared more sumptuously than the cupbearer of the French. After some time, letters were forged in the tent of the King of the French, by which, as if they had been sent by his nobles out of France, the King was recalled to his own country."

And so Philip of France, amid oaths and protestations of faith to Richard, sailed for Europe. "How faithfully he kept his oath the whole world knows. For directly he reached home, he stirred up the whole land and threw Normandy into confusion. What need for further words! Amid the curses of all, he departed, leaving his army at Acre."

CHAPTER XII

The Adventures of Richard Lion-Heart

One who fought his fight has told the deeds
Of that gay passage through the midland sea
Cyprus and Sicily;
And how the Lion-Heart o'er the Moslem host
Triumphed in Ascalon
Or Acre, by the tideless Syrian coast.

PALGRAVE: *Visions of England.*

Exactly two years after the siege of Acre had commenced, the army of Richard, together with the Knights of the Temple and the Hospital, set out to conquer the territory that lay between the mountains and the sea.

And "as the army marched along the sea-shore that was in its right, all the while the Turks watched its movements from the heights on the left." The progress of the Crusaders was therefore one long battle, and it was further harassed by the natural difficulties of the road. "That day," says Geoffrey de Vinsauf, an eye-witness of these things, "the army moved forward with more than wonted caution, and stopped, after a long march, impeded by the thickets and the tall and luxuriant herbage, which struck them in the face. In these maritime parts there were also a number of beasts of the forest, who leapt up between their feet from the long grass and thick copses."

He tells us, moreover, of the touching device employed to stir the hearts of the wearied soldiers, and to remind them of the aim of their journey.

"It was the custom of the army each night before lying down to rest to depute some one to stand in the middle of the camp and cry out with a loud voice, 'Help! Help! for the Holy Sepulchre!' The rest of the army took it up and repeated the words, and stretching their hands to heaven, prayed for the mercy and assistance of God in the cause. Then the herald himself repeated in a loud voice: 'Help! Help! for the Holy Sepulchre!' and everyone repeated it after him a second and a third time. The army," he adds naïvely, "appeared to be much refreshed by crying out in this fashion."

At length the preliminary skirmishes gave place to a pitched battle, of which our eye-witness gives a spirited account.

"On the Saturday, the Eve of the Nativity of the Blessed Virgin Mary, at earliest dawn, our men armed themselves with great care to receive the Turks, who were known to have preceded their march, and whose insolence nothing but a battle could check.... On that day the Templars formed the first rank, and after them came in due order the Bretons and men of Anjou; then followed King Guy with the men of Poitou; in the fourth line were the Normans and English who had the care of the royal standard; and last of all marched the Hospitallers: this line was composed of chosen warriors, divided into companies.

"They kept together so closely that an apple, if thrown, would not have fallen to the ground without touching a man or a horse; and the army stretched from the army of the Saracens to the seashore. There you might have seen standards and ensigns of various forms, and hardy warriors, fresh and full of spirits and well fitted for war.

"King Richard and the Duke of Burgundy, with a chosen retinue of warriors, rode up and down, narrowly watching the position and manner of the Turks, to correct anything in their own troops if they saw occasion.

"It was now nearly nine o'clock, when there appeared a large body of the Turks, ten thousand strong, coming down upon us at full charge, and throwing darts and arrows, as fast as they could, while they mingled their voices in one horrible yell.

"There followed after them an infernal race of men, of black colour.... With them also were the Saracens who live in the desert, called Bedouins; they are a savage race of men, blacker than soot; they fight on foot and carry a bow, quiver and round shield, and are a light and active race.

"These men dauntlessly attacked our army. They came on with irresistible charge, on horses swifter than eagles, and urged on like lightning to attack our men; and as they advanced they raised a cloud of dust, so that the sky was darkened. In front came certain of their admirals, as was their duty, with clarions and trumpets; some had horns, others had pipes and timbrels, gongs, cymbals and other instruments, producing a horrible noise and clamour. This they did to excite their spirits and courage, for the more violent the clamour became the more bold were they for the fray."

So hot grew the contest, and such was the inconvenience suffered by the Crusaders because of their narrow quarters between the foe and the sea, that there was nothing for it but to retreat. This of course brought the full force of the attack upon the Hospitallers, "the more so," says Geoffrey, "as they were unable to resist, but moved forward with patience under their wounds, returning not even a word for the blows which fell upon them, and advancing on their way because they were not able to bear the weight of the contest.

"A cloud of dust obscured the air as our men marched on; and in addition to the heat, they had an enemy pressing them in the rear, insolent and rendered obstinate by the instigation of the devil. Still the Christians proved good men, and secure in their unconquerable spirit, kept constantly advancing, while the Turks threatened them without ceasing in the rear; but their blows fells harmless upon the defensive armour, and this caused the Turks to slacken in courage at the failure of their attempts, and they began to murmur in disappointment, crying out in their rage 'that our people were of iron and would yield to no blow.'

"Then the Turks, about twenty thousand strong, rushed again upon our men pell-mell, annoying them in every possible manner, when, as if almost overcome by their savage fury, Brother Gamier, one of the Hospitallers, suddenly exclaimed with a loud voice, 'O excellent St George! Will you leave us to be thus put to confusion? The whole of Christendom is now on the point of perishing, because it fears to return a blow against this impious race.'"

The King, however, had determined that no charge should be made until the army had, by retreat, obtained a better position for so doing. So, even when the Grand Master of the Hospitallers went to him, and said, "My lord the king, we are violently pressed by the enemy, and are in danger of eternal infamy, as if we did not dare to return their blows. We are each of us losing our horses one after another, and why should we bear with them any further?" The King replied, "Good Master, it is you who must sustain their attack; no one could be everywhere at once."

"On the Master returning, the Turks again made a fierce attack upon them from the rear, and there was not a prince or count among them but blushed with shame and said to each other, 'Why do we not charge them at full gallop? Alas! Alas! we shall for ever deserve to be called cowards, a thing which never happened to us before, for never has such a disgrace befallen so great an army, even from the unbelievers. Unless we defend ourselves by immediately charging the enemy, we shall gain everlasting scandal, and so much the greater the longer we delay to fight.'"

In spite of these protests, they had all come to the conclusion that the King was right in not ordering them to charge till all were in a more advantageous position, when "the success of the affair was marred," says Geoffrey, "by two knights who were impatient of delay." Fortunately, Richard, seeing the mistake in time, gave the order, "Prepare to charge!" forthwith. "The sky grew black with the dust that was raised in the confusion of that encounter. The Turks who had purposely dismounted from their horses in order to take better aim at our men with their darts and arrows, were slain on all sides in that charge. King Richard, on seeing his army in motion and in encounter with the Turks, flew rapidly on his horse through the Hospitallers who had led the charge, and to whom he was bringing assistance with all his retinue, and broke into the Turkish infantry, who were astonished at his blows and those of his men, and gave way to the right and to the left."

A terrific fight ensued, ending in a triumph for the Crusaders in so far that they had scattered the foe and were able to proceed upon their march in safety.

In equally vivid phrase Geoffrey describes the anger of Saladin when the news reached him of this defeat. Bitterly did he reproach and deride his men, while his "admirals" listened with heads bowed down. At last one bolder than the rest made answer, "Most sacred Sultan, saving your Majesty, this charge is unjust, for we fought with all our strength and did our best to destroy them. We met their fiercest attacks, but it was of no avail. They are armed in impenetrable armour which no weapon can pierce so that our blows fell as it were upon a rock of flint. And further, there is one among their number superior to any man we have ever seen; he always charges before the rest, slaying and destroying our men. He is the first in every enterprise, and is a most brave and excellent soldier; no one can resist him or escape out of his hands. They call him *Melech Ric* (King Richard). Such a king as he seems born to command the whole earth; what then could we do more against so formidable an enemy?"

Such is the description which Geoffrey, in his hero-worship, puts into the mouth of the vanquished leaders of the Saracens, and Saladin, no longer making light of the danger that threatened his realm, promptly destroyed all his more important fortresses, such as Joppa and Ascalon, for fear *Melech Ric* should occupy them.

Richard himself was now very anxious to get possession of Ascalon, and to re-fortify the walls. But on this point opinions were divided. The French were, as usual, violently opposed to him, and wanted rather to rebuild the fort of Joppa, "because it furnished a shorter and easier route for pilgrims going to Jerusalem," and the feeling of the multitude was with them.

Richard of England utterly defeats Saladin

"Foolish counsel; fatal obstinacy of those indolent men!" comments Geoffrey. "By providing for their immediate comfort and to avoid labour and expense, they did what they would afterwards repent of, for had they then saved Ascalon from the Turks, the whole land would soon have been clear of them. But the cry of the people prevailed, a collection was made, and they immediately began to rebuild the towers, and to clear out the moat of Joppa. The army remained there long, enjoying ease and pleasure ... and the whole people became corrupted; the zeal of pilgrimage waxed cold, and all their works of devotion were neglected."

It was about this time that an adventure befel King Richard which nearly put an end to his career as leader of the Third Crusade.

"About this time," says Geoffrey, "King Richard went out hawking with a small escort, intending, if he saw any small body of Turks, to fall upon them.

"Fatigued by his ride, he fell asleep, and a troop of the enemy rushed suddenly upon him to make him prisoner. The King, awakened by the noise, had barely time to mount his bay Cyprian horse, and his attendants were still in the act of mounting, when the Turks came upon them and tried to take him; but the King, drawing his sword, rushed upon them, and they, pretending flight, drew him after them to a place where there was another body of Turks in ambush. These started up with speed, and surrounded the King in order to make him prisoner. The King defended himself bravely, and the enemy drew back, though he would certainly have been captured if the Turks had known who he was.

"But in the midst of the conflict, one of the King's companions, William de Pratelles, called out in the Saracen language that *he* was the "Melech," *i.e.* the King; and the Turks, believing what he said, led him off captive to their own army.

"At the news of this action our army was alarmed, and seizing their arms, came at full gallop to find the King, and when they met him returning safe, he faced about and with them pursued the Turks, who had carried off William de Pratelles thinking they had got the King. They could not, however, overtake the fugitives, and King

Richard, reserved by the Divine Hand for greater things, returned to the camp, to the great joy of his soldiers, who thanked God for his preservation, but grieved for William de Pratelles, who loyally redeemed the King at the price of his own liberty."

Richard was much blamed by some of his friends for his rashness on this occasion. "But," says Geoffrey the hero-worshipper, "notwithstanding these admonitions on the part of his best friends, the King's nature still broke out; in all expeditions he was the first to advance and the last to retreat; and he never failed, either by his own valour or the Divine Aid, to bring back numbers of captives, or, if they resisted, to put them to the sword."

When the fortress of Joppa had been rebuilt, Richard sent a "distinguished embassy" to Saladin and Saphadim, his brother, to demand the surrender of the Holy Land once more. This was to include the whole kingdom of Syria, as well as tribute for Babylon, and to this Saladin would not agree. At the same time he appeared to deal very reasonably with the embassy, sending back with them his brother Saphadim, and offering through him to give up the kingdom of Jerusalem "from the Jordan to the sea," on condition that the city Ascalon should never be rebuilt. The account of the meeting of the two great representatives of Christendom and Islam is very interesting, and the more so because Richard never came face to face with the renowned Saladin himself.

"When Saphadim came with this message to the King, Richard, who had just been bled, would not converse with him on that day; but he was supplied with every kind of delicacy for his table, and entertained in the valley between the castles of the Temple and Jehoshaphat.

"The next day Saphadim sent a present of seven camels and a rich tent, and coming into the King's presence, delivered Saladin's message, upon which Richard determined to have patience for a time, that he might the better make provision for the future. But, alas! he showed too little prudence in not foreseeing the deceit with which they sought to protract the time until the cities, castles and fortresses of that country were destroyed.

"In short, Saphadim so cunningly beguiled the too credulous king, that one would have thought they had contracted a mutual friendship; for the King received Saphadim's gifts, and messengers were daily passing with presents to the King, much to the annoyance of his friends. But Saphadim pleaded that he wished to make peace between them, and the King thought he was adopting a wise policy, by which the bounds of Christianity would be enlarged, and a creditable peace concluded.

"When, however, the King discovered that the promises of Saphadim were mere words, he at once broke off the negotiations."

The Saracens said in after days that Richard's friendship with Saphadim went so far that he offered him his sister Joanna in marriage; but that Joanna herself refused with scorn to marry an infidel.

It was not until nearly the end of that year, when much time had been lost, that the army of Richard once more turned its face towards Jerusalem. The Templars however, tried to prevent the King from attempting the siege of the Holy City, "lest, while they were besieging Saladin and the garrison, the Turkish army which was outside among the mountains, might attack our men by surprise, and so place them between the attack of the garrison from within and the Turkish army from without."

But Richard was sick and tired of inaction, and his army had been lately much depressed by the miserable weather of winter.

The rain and the hail had killed many of their beasts of burden; storms had torn up the pegs of the tents, drowned the horses and spoiled all their biscuits and bacon. "Their clothes were dissolved by the wet, and the men themselves suffered from the unwonted severity of the climate."

"Under all those sufferings, their only consolation arose from their zeal in the service of God, and a desire to finish their pilgrimage. Even those who were sick in bed at Joppa were carried in litters, so great was their wish to see Jerusalem."

But the weather grew worse, and at length the advice of the Templars, experienced as they were in that climate, prevailed.

Most of the French went back to Joppa, and with much wrath on the part of Richard and deep despondency on the part of his army, a march was made instead upon the ruined town of Ascalon.

At the end of January, however, "the sky became brighter," and many of the French were induced to return to Richard, and to help him to rebuild the walls. But very soon the old quarrels broke out.

The Duke of Burgundy, finding himself without the means to pay his men, asked King Richard to supply him with a large sum of money, as he had done once before at Acre. When the King refused, on the ground that his previous loan had never been repaid, the duke at once left Ascalon, taking his army with him, and went back to Acre.

About the same time Conrad of Tyre gave mortal offence to Richard by his refusal to come to help him to rebuild the city, and the King, in his wrath, began to make fresh attempts at peace with Saladin, on the plea that his foeman was of nobler mettle than his so-called allies. Friendly overtures went so far that "on Palm Sunday, King Richard, amid much splendour, girded with the belt of knighthood the son of Saphadim, who had been sent to him for that purpose."

After Easter, came bad news from England to the King—news of the treachery of his brother John, of the seizing of the revenues, and of an empty treasury.

"And if," said the prior of Hereford who brought this news, "your majesty does not take speedy counsel on these matters, and return home with all haste and avenge our wrongs on the insurgents, it will fare worse, and you will not be able to recover your kingdom without the hazard of a war."

When these things were laid before the leaders of the army, as a reason why Richard must speedily return to his own land, they unanimously declared that something must be done to settle affairs in Palestine by choosing a king, "one whom the army could follow and obey," and that if this were not done "they would one and all depart from the land, for they should not otherwise be able to guard against the enemy." The choice was given them between Guy of Lusignan and Conrad of Tyre, and to the secret disgust of Richard, they chose the latter, "as being much better able to defend the country."

The King gave his consent, though with no good will, for the Marquis Conrad was known to be in league with Saladin, who, on his part, was inclined to treat with him against the advice of Saphadim, who would do nothing "without King Richard's consent."

Conrad himself was delighted at the news that the crown was his if he would but do his best against the foe, and his followers at Tyre indulged, says Geoffrey, in a joy "the more unreasonable for being so intemperate."

Then came a tragedy, swift and sudden. The marquis was returning one day in a very cheerful and pleasant humour, from an entertainment given by the Bishop of Beauvais, at which he had been a guest, and had reached the Custom House of the city, when two young men, without cloaks, suddenly rushed upon him, and having drawn their daggers, stabbed him to the heart and ran off at full speed.

"The marquis instantly fell from his horse and rolled dying on the ground; one of the murderers was slain directly, but the second took shelter in a church, notwithstanding which he was captured and condemned to be dragged through the city until life should be extinct.

"Now while the marquis was breathing his last, the attendants who were about him, took him up in their arms, and carried him to the palace, mourning and weeping inconsolably, the more so as their joy had been, but now, so great. He enjoined his wife to attend carefully to the preservation of the city of Tyre, and to resign it to no one, save King Richard. Immediately afterwards he died, and was buried in the Hospital amidst great mourning and lamentation.

Thus the cheering hopes of that desolate land were destroyed, and the former gladness was turned into intense grief.

With great treachery the French now began to spread abroad a report that Richard himself "had vilely brought about the death of the marquis," an accusation for which there was no shadow of proof. Not content with this, the French army, which lived in tents outside the city sent orders to Queen Isabella, the wife of Conrad, "bidding her place the city in their charge, without delay or opposition, for the service of the King of France. But she, mindful of the dying words of her lord, replied that when King Richard came to see her, she would give it up to him and to none other, as there was no one who had laboured so much to rescue the Holy Land from the hands of the Turks."

The French were very indignant at this reply, and while they were attempting to gain possession of the city, Count Henry of Champagne, the nephew of Richard, arrived unexpectedly on the scene.

"And when the people saw him among them, they forthwith chose him as their prince, as if he had been sent by God; and began with much earnestness to entreat him to accept the crown of the kingdom, without excuse or hesitation, and to marry the widow of the marquis, as the kingdom was hers by right of inheritance." To this Richard willingly agreed, and thus Henry became the nominal king of Jerusalem, while the Holy City remained in the hands of Islam.

The sympathy of our chronicler Geoffrey is, however, entirely with the deposed Guy of Lusignan, "who," says he "now dwelt within the kingdom like a private man, not because he was undeserving, but for this only reason—that he was simple-minded and unversed in political intrigue. Thus then Guy became a king without a kingdom, until King Richard, moved with pity for him, gave him the unconditional sovereignty of the island of Cyprus."

Further news of the disturbed state of his own kingdom at home now arrived for Richard, but, in spite of this, he was persuaded without much difficulty to defer his return until the Easter of the following year, by which time it was hoped that Jerusalem would have been taken.

This intelligence was proclaimed throughout the army by means of a herald, "and when the army heard it, they were as delighted as a bird at dawn of day, and all immediately set themselves in readiness, packing up their luggage and preparing for the march."

After a few days journey, a halt was called until Count Henry could join them with the rest of the army from Acre, and this delay enabled Richard to seize a richly loaded caravan, an event which caused something like a panic among the Turks. "Never," says one of them, "did any news so trouble the Sultan."

But the English King was only too well aware of the real weakness of his army, and when the soldiers urged him to march directly upon the Holy City, he firmly refused.

"If it pleases you to proceed to Jerusalem," he said to the other leaders, "I will not desert you; I will be your comrade but not your commander; I will follow, not lead you. Does not Saladin know all that goes on in our camp? And do you think that our weak condition has escaped his notice?"

This was the occasion of great discontent among the Crusaders. In vain did the King propose to attack the power of Islam in Cairo or Damascus; the French declared that they would march only against Jerusalem, from which they were now but four miles distant. Quarrels arose among the soldiers, some taking one side, some the other, and finally the army retreated, in separate divisions and in a very depressed state, to Joppa, and thence to Acre.

We may well believe that the heaviest heart in all that company was that of the King himself. They tell us that in his pursuit of a party of Turks near Emmaus, Richard found himself upon a hill from which he could catch a glimpse of the Holy City in the distance. Turning away his eyes, he cried out with tears that he was not worthy even to look upon the spot which he had failed to wrest from the hand of the infidel; and so he retraced his steps in sadness to the sea-shore.

The retreat of the army from Joppa was an opportunity not to be lost by the astute Saladin. Whilst Richard was vainly trying to patch up a truce with him from Acre, the Sultan swooped down on the unprotected walls of Joppa and took the city after a five days' siege.

This news of the arrival of Saladin reached Acre just as Richard was preparing to sail to his own land. He immediately set off with fifty knights in two or three galleys and being detained by contrary winds, reached the city only to find the banners of Saladin floating from the walls, and all the city save one tower in his hands. Dashing through the waves to the shore, Richard led his little band to the gates of the city, forced his way in, tore down the flag of Islam and hoisted his own in its stead.

"Saladin, hearing of the King's arrival, and of his brilliant contest with the Turks, of whom he had slain all who opposed him, was seized with sudden fear, and like that timid animal the hare, put spurs to his horse, and fled before his face."

Presently, however, it dawned upon him that instead of having been attacked by a great army from Acre, he had been routed by a mere handful of men, most of whom were now sleeping unprotected in camp.

"But a certain Genoese was led by the divine impulse to go out early in the morning into the fields, where he was alarmed by the noise of men and horses advancing, and returned speedily, but just had time to see helmets reflecting back the light which now fell upon them. He immediately rushed with speed into the camp, calling out "To arms! To arms!"

The King was awakened by the noise, and leaping startled from his bed, put on his coat of mail and summoned his men to the rescue.

During the battle that followed, in which Richard is said to have performed almost incredible deeds of valour, Saphadim showed him an example of generosity and courtesy.

The King had been unhorsed and was fighting desperately on foot when "a Turk advanced towards him mounted on a prancing steed.

He had been sent by Saphadim, who now sent to the King as a token of his well known honourable character, two noble horses, requesting him earnestly to accept them and make use of them, and if he returned safe and sound out of that battle, to remember the gifts and to recompense it in any way he pleased."

This was the last battle fought and the last victory won by Richard in the Holy Land. He himself fell ill from the fatigue of that day, the French refused to fight any more under his leadership, and England and Normandy were clamouring for his return.

So he employed Saphadim, always kindly disposed towards him, to intercede with Saladin for a truce; and this was finally agreed upon for the space of three years, the Christians meantime holding Joppa and Tyre, and all the land between; and all pilgrims having the right to visit Jerusalem in safety.

But the Holy City remained yet in the hands of the infidel, and the Third Crusade had come to an end before its real work had been begun.

Well might Richard gaze upon the land with heavy heart as he set sail for Europe.

"All night the ship ran on her way by the light of the stars, and when morning dawned, the King looked back with yearning eyes upon the land he had left; and after long meditation he prayed aloud in these words.

"O Holy Land, I commend thee to God, and if His heavenly grace shall grant me so long to live, that I may, in His good pleasure, afford thee assistance, I hope, as I propose, to be able to be some day a succour to thee."

But though he had not yet come to the end of his adventures in connection with it, the deeds of Richard, in the Holy Land he loved, were over.

He had sent on his wife and sister in front, and they had reached Sicily in safety, whilst he himself set out in a single vessel, only to meet with such stormy winds, that he found himself at length a shipwrecked stranger on that strip of the Istrian coast that borders the Adriatic Sea.

It was an unlucky spot for Richard. The governor of the district was Maynard, a nephew of that Conrad of Tyre of whose death the English King was held to be guilty.

Nor was Vienna very far off—Vienna ruled by Leopold of Austria, his ancient foe. But Richard's beard had been allowed to grow of late, and pilgrims' dresses were not difficult to obtain for himself and his companion, Baldwin of Bethune.

Making his way to the Castle of Maynard, with his usual rashness he bade Baldwin win his way to the governor by the gift of a magnificent ruby ring taken from his own finger, and ask of him a passport for the two, Baldwin and "Hugh the Merchant," as for pilgrims making their way back through the province from Jerusalem.

Long did Maynard gaze upon the jewel, until at length he said "This jewel can come only from a king; and that king can only be Richard of England. Bid him come to me in peace."

But Richard would not enter the lion's cage. He fled in the night to Friesach, leaving Baldwin and his other companions to be seized as hostages and kept in bonds. Travelling about the country with one knight as his comrade, together with a boy who could speak the language, Richard drew nearer and nearer to the dangerous region of Vienna.

Resting in the inn of a town close by the capital, he sent the boy to buy food for their journey in the marketplace. The lad chose to swagger and boast of his master's wealth and mysterious high position, in proof of which he pulled out a handful of gold coins before the bystanders.

This was the cause of his immediate discomfiture, for he was seized, carried before the chief man of the district and questioned as to whom he served.

He refused to disclose the name of his master, and was put to the torture. This was no light matter in those rough days, and under it the boy confessed that he was the page of Richard of England.

The news was carried hotfoot to Leopold, and meantime a troop of armed men surrounded the inn where lay the unsuspecting monarch.

Richard, however, was never to be caught with ease. Sword in hand he defended himself with such vigour that the men fell back. Escape was hopeless, notwithstanding this pause, and the King at length agreed to yield if their chief would come in person to take him.

But this chief turned out to be Leopold of Austria himself, grimly delighted to find his former foe within his clutches. Other forces were also at work to get possession of the person of the English King. Philip of France had not forgotten his ancient grudge against him; and it was to his advantage that Richard's return to England should be hindered, since he intended meantime to annex Normandy. John, the King's brother, would now have his chance of obtaining the coveted English crown, and so it was to the interest of all his enemies to keep him safe within prison walls. But a yet more powerful enemy was in league with both, and only too ready to take revenge upon Richard for the part he had once played in taking the side of Tancred of Sicily against him. The Emperor Henry VI. son of Barbarossa, offered Leopold a bribe of £60,000 for the person of the King, and Richard found himself closely confined in a lonely castle of the Tyrol, the prisoner of the Emperor.

For a while no one knew of his place of concealment, nor into whose hands he had fallen.

At length, says the romantic story, this was discovered by his faithful minstrel, Blondel, who travelled over Eastern Europe, searching and inquiring for his master. One day, as he sat beneath the walls of a castle keep, he began to play upon his lute one of the troubadour airs that Richard had loved to sing in former days. To his surprise, the song was softly echoed from the walls. Staying only long enough to make sure that it was his beloved master, the minstrel sped back with the news to England.

This charming story may have no foundation save in the fact that the English Chancellor, William Longchamp, in his wish to leave no stone unturned in the attempt to discover the King, sent out messengers of all ranks and degrees on his behalf. Whoever found out his place of imprisonment matters little; for, directly it was known, all the powers of Christendom were set on foot to work the release of one who had done so much for the cause of God in the Holy Land.

The Pope brought pressure to bear upon the Emperor; the Emperor consented to accept a ransom for his royal captive, in spite of the fact that John of England had offered him twenty thousand pounds for every month that Richard could be kept in prison; and the hard-pressed English people once more brought out their coins on behalf of a King whose eastern expeditions had already cost them dear.

And thus at length the adventures of the Lion Heart in connection with the Third Crusade came to an end.

CHAPTER XIII

The Story of Dandolo the Blind Doge; or, The Fourth and Fifth Crusades

Oh for one hour of blind old Dandolo!
Th'octogenarian chief, Byzantium's conquering foe.

BYRON: *Childe Harold.*

Richard the Lion-Heart had returned to England in 1194. The next three years of the dying century saw an attempt at an expedition sometimes known as the Fourth, more often as the "German" Crusade.

Its story contains little of interest. Saladin had died before the release of Richard, and his brother Saphadim reigned in his stead, when Henry, Emperor of Germany, hoping to win the favour of his disapproving subjects, sent an expedition to the Holy Land.

The Christian lords who yet held rule in Palestine had found things run so smoothly under the hand of the Sultan during the long truce, that they were in no hurry to break the peace. But the Germans did not mean to wait for their assistance, and while they were marshalling their forces, Saphadim drew first blood by a sudden and successful attack upon Joppa, once so ably held and fortified by Richard.

The German Crusaders retaliated by a victory or rather a series of victories, which restored to them Joppa and many other coast towns, and augured well for the future. All this, however, was undone by their own cruelty and thirst for blood.

On their triumphant march to Jerusalem they were besieging a certain castle, and had succeeded in tunnelling passages through the rock upon which it stood. Hopeless of escape, the Moslem garrison offered to surrender on condition that they were allowed a safe passage into their own territory. To this the Crusaders agreed, but a certain number of them were loud in their disapproval, and began to threaten the Saracens to such an extent that the latter lost faith in the promises that had been given. Declaring that they would die rather than submit, they lined the newly-cut rock-passages and prepared to sell their lives dearly.

The Crusaders, furious at their defiant message, dashed into the dark tunnels, only to fall by thousands at the hands of their unseen and desperate foes. Nightfall saw them repulsed and utterly dismayed at the unexpected resistance; discipline was gone, none knew what to do next. Then followed a disgraceful breach of honour. Their leaders stole away under cover of the darkness, and the German soldiers found themselves left at the mercy of the foe.

Fortunately for them, the Saracens were too exhausted to pursue their advantage, and the Germans, leaving their baggage and even their weapons behind them, fled in disorder to Tyre.

The news of the death of their Emperor recalled most of these faint-hearted Soldiers of the Cross to Germany.

The remainder made one last endeavour to fortify Joppa and entrench themselves within it; but, in the November of 1197, the city fell before a furious attack of the Saracens, and the greater part of the inhabitants were slaughtered.

This was the sad and disgraceful end of the Fourth Crusade, which left the Latin Kingdom of Jerusalem a kingdom only in name.

The Fifth Crusade is remarkable for the fact that it began in an outburst of keen religious enthusiasm, and ended in a riot of cruelty, bloodshed and profanity, without ever reaching the Holy Land at all.

Two very different men were responsible for stirring up this Crusade in Europe. Innocent the Third, one of the youngest, most energetic and most ambitious of popes, thought to find in it an opportunity of increasing his "temporal" as well as spiritual power.

It had long been the custom for princes, going forth on perilous adventure, to leave their lands in charge of the Holy Father; and even if this were not always done, the Crusades gave many a chance of interfering with the affairs of kingdoms and dukedoms whose people were engaged in the great religious war.

Apart from this, the young Pope was, like all enthusiasts in religion, deeply affected by the idea of the unhappy state of the Holy Land, and sincerely desired to stir the hearts of the princes of Europe to do their part towards restoring it to Christendom. But the princes of Europe had had enough of Crusades and they turned a deaf ear to the call. It needed another Peter the Hermit, or at least another St Bernard to stir the hearts of rich and poor to march forth once more upon a quest that had cost them already so dear.

Then the right man appeared upon the scene. A certain French priest, Fulk by name, in atonement for a life of carelessness and sin, began to preach the duty of taking up the Cross in the Holy War. A mere village *curé*, he was content at first to teach and speak only in his own neighbourhood, but his reputation increased, he became noted as a worker of miracles, and rumours about him ere long reached the ears of the Pope. Innocent III. quickly saw in him the instrument he needed. Throughout the streets and slums of Paris, in castle and in cottage, Fulk was encouraged to make his way, calling upon men to repent of their sins and to atone for them by taking up arms for the Cause of Christ.

As usual, "the common people heard him gladly," while for a time the nobles ignored him.

Then it came to pass that young Count Theobald of Champagne held a great tournament, at which assembled two thousand knights. Into the midst of that gay throng appeared on a sudden the inspired face of Fulk the priest, dressed in his threadbare cassock. His burning words carried conviction to the hearts of the knights, and Theobald himself was the first to take up the Cross. Others followed—amongst them Simon de Montfort, father of the famous "good Earl Simon" of English history—and finally nearly all that great band of knights were enlisted as Crusaders.

Everywhere the same result was seen. Great sums of money were raised for the enterprise. Louis, Count of Blois, and Baldwin, Count of Flanders, joined the band of leaders, and while preparations went on apace in France, Baldwin mindful of the chief reason for past failures, sent a message to Dandolo, the blind Doge of Venice, asking him to supply flat-bottomed boats in which {163} for a certain sum of money, the Crusading armies might be transported to the Holy Land.

One of those sent upon this mission was Geoffrey de Villehardouin, Marshal of Champagne, who tells the story of this, the Fifth Crusade, so vividly.

"The Doge of Venice," says he, "whose name was Henry Dandolo, and who was very wise and very valiant, did them (the envoys) great honour, and entertained them right willingly, marvelling, however, what might be the matter that had brought them to that country. The envoys entered the palace, which was passing rich and beautiful, and found the Doge and his council in a chamber.

"There they delivered their message after this manner. 'Sire, we come to thee on the part of the high barons of France who have taken the Sign of the Cross to avenge the shame done to Jesus Christ and to reconquer Jerusalem, if so be that God will suffer it. And because they know that no people have such great power to help them as you and your people, therefore we pray you by God that you take pity on the land oversea, and the shame of Christ, and use diligence that our lords have ships for transport and battle.'

"'And after what manner should we use diligence?' said the Doge.

"'After all manner that you may advise and propose,' rejoined the envoys, 'in so far as what you propose may be within our means.'

"'Certes,' said the Doge, 'it is a great thing that your lords require of us, and well it seems that they have in view a high enterprise. We will give you our answer eight days from to-day, for it is meet so great a matter be fully pondered.'"

So eight days later, when the covenant had been proposed and accepted by the council and the envoys, a "mass of the Holy Ghost was celebrated in the chapel of St Mark, 'the most beautiful chapel that there is.' To this gathered 'well ten thousand of the people,' and immediately afterwards the French envoys were bidden 'to humbly ask them to assent to the proposed covenant.'

"Villehardouin himself was spokesman before that multitude, and said unto them. 'Lords, the barons of France, most high and puissant, have sent us to you, and they cry to you for mercy, that you have pity on Jerusalem, which is in bondage to the Turks, and that for God's sake, you help to avenge the shame of Christ Jesus.

"And for this end they have elected to come to you, because they know full well that there is none other people having so great power on the seas as you and your people. And they commanded us to fall at your feet, and not to rise till you consent to take pity on the Holy Land which is beyond the seas.'

"Then the six envoys knelt at the feet of the people, weeping many tears. And the Doge and all the others burst into tears of pity and compassion, and cried with one voice, and lifted up their hands, saying: 'We consent! We consent!'

"Then was there so great a noise and tumult that it seemed as if the earth itself were falling to pieces.

"And when this great tumult and passion of pity—greater did never any man see—were appeased, the Good Doge of Venice, who was very wise and valiant, went up into the reading-desk, and spoke to the people, and said to them:

"'Signors, behold the honour that God has done you, for the best people in the world have set aside all other people, and chosen you to join them in so high an enterprise as the deliverance of our Lord.'"

Thus comes on the stage upon which was played the story of the Fifth Crusade, that curious and interesting figure, the blind old Doge, Henry Dandolo, who, for all intents and purposes, may be regarded as the leader of that expedition, so completely did he sway its designs by his counsel and action.

Years before, or so the story goes, he had been sent on an embassy to Constantinople, and there had been seized and treacherously ill-used so that he became practically blind. Whether this is true or not, the fact remains that Dandolo hated the Greeks with a bitter hatred, and was ready to use any means towards their hurt or downfall.

So the treaty was made, and the Crusaders promised to pay the whole expenses of the expedition, a sum amounting to eighty-five thousand pieces of silver, on condition that they were provided food and transport. And to show their goodwill, the Venetians added fifty armed galleys to the fleet, "for the love of God."

Then the envoys returned rejoicing, only to meet with one piece of ill luck after another.

On his journey to Champagne, Geoffrey de Villehardouin met a large company of men, amongst whom were several important barons who had taken the Cross, and who were now following Walter of Brienne on an expedition to conquer the land of his wife, the daughter of King Tancred of Sicily.

"Now when he told them the news how the envoys had fared, great was their joy, and much did they prize the arrangements made. And they said, 'We are already on our way; and when you come, you will find us ready.'"

"But," comments Geoffrey somewhat wearily, for this was but the first of many wasteful and irregular expeditions, "events fall out as God wills, and never had they power to join the host. This was much to our loss, for they were of great prowess and valiant." And then they parted and each went on his way.

The next blow hit Geoffrey very hard. He rode day by day so that he came at length, he says, to Troyes, in Champagne, and found his lord, Count Theobald, sick and languishing, and right glad was the Count at his coming. And when he had told him how he fared, Theobald was so rejoiced that he said he would mount his horse, a thing he had not done for a long time. So he rose from his bed and rode forth. "But alas: how great the pity! For never again did he bestride horse but that once."

Growing worse and worse, the Count began to realise that his part in the Crusade was over. So he divided the money which would have taken him on pilgrimage among his followers and companions, giving orders that each one, on receiving it, should swear "on holy relics, to join the host at Venice."

"Many there were," says Geoffrey, "who kept that oath badly and so incurred great blame."

So the Count Theobald died and was buried, and the Crusaders looked about them for another chief. First they went to Odo, Duke of Burgundy, his cousin, and offered him their faith and loyalty. "But such was his pleasure that he refused. And be it known to you that he might have done much better," is the terse comment of Geoffrey.

Finally, Boniface, Marquis of Montferrat, one of the foremost nobles in that land, a patron of poets and troubadours and a skilled soldier, received the "lordship of the host."

"Whereupon the Bishop of Soissons, and Master Fulk, that holy man, and two white monks whom the Marquis had brought with him from his own land, led him into the church of Notre Dame at Soissons, and attached the Cross to his shoulder."

The death of Theobald was not the last blow that fate had in store for the Crusaders, says Geoffrey. "Thus did the pilgrims make ready in all lands. Alas! A great mischance befell them in the following Lent, before they had started, for another notable chief, Count Geoffrey of Perche, fell sick, and made his will in such fashion that he directed that Stephen, his brother, should have his goods and lead his men in the host. Of this exchange the pilgrims would willingly have been quit, had God so ordered. Thus did the Count make an end and die; and much evil ensued, for he was a baron high and honoured, and a good knight. Greatly was he mourned throughout all lands."

It was soon after the Easter of 1202 that the French Crusaders began their march. Fulk himself, the originator of the movement, did not accompany them, remaining behind, possibly to stir up fresh enthusiasm and supplies of money if not of men. But he was not destined to see with his bodily eyes the failure of the expedition, for he died of fever at Neuilly, while the pilgrims were still at Venice.

The French army marched by way of the Jura Mountains and through Lombardy, where they were joined by the Marquis of Montferrat with his troops of Lombards, Piedmontese and Savoyards, and by a small band of Germans.

At the same time a fleet had started from Flanders, the leaders of which had promised Count Baldwin to join the Crusaders at Venice.

"But ill did these keep the faith they had sworn to the Count, they and others like them, because they, and such others of the same sort, became fearful of the great perils that the host of Venice had undertaken."

Many of the French leaders, too, failed the main body of the Crusaders in the same way; for they avoided the passage to Venice because of the danger, and went instead to Marseilles, "whereof," says Geoffrey, "they received shame and much were they blamed—and great were the mishaps that afterwards befell them."

Meantime, the French army, under the Marquis of Montferrat, had arrived safely at Venice, and was rejoiced to see the fair array of ships and transports waiting to convey it to the Holy Land.

But now an unexpected difficulty arose; for, of all that great number of barons who had sworn to bring their men to Venice, only a very few had arrived; and then came the disconcerting news that many of these pilgrims were travelling by other ways and from other ports.

Consternation ensued among the barons, for the Venetians were naturally determined that the money stipulated for the transports should be paid at once, and this could only be done if all the barons bore their share, as they had agreed to do.

So envoys, amongst whom was again found Geoffrey de Villehardouin, were sent to intercept the various leaders of armies, and "to beseech them to have pity on the Holy Land beyond the sea, and show them that no other passages save that from Venice could be of profit."

These envoys met with only partial success. Count Louis of Blois agreed to accompany them, but many others chose to go their own way. "And then," says Geoffrey, "was the host of those who went by Venice greatly weakened, and much evil befell them therefrom, as you shall shortly hear."

The Venetians had done their part well. They "held a market" for the Crusaders, "rich and abundant, of all things needful for horses and men. And the fleet they had got ready was so goodly and fine that never did Christian man see one goodlier or finer; both galleys and transports; and sufficient for at least three times as many men as were in the host."

The first difficulty arose, naturally, over the matter of payment. Each man had done what he could, but the total sum came to less than half of that which was due.

Earnestly did the barons urge the need of making further payment in fulfilment of their promise. "For God's sake," said they, "let each contribute all that he has, so that we may fulfil our covenant; for better it is that we should lose all that we have than lose what we have already paid and prove false to our promises; for if this host remains here, the rescue of the land oversea comes to naught."

But the other barons and the lesser folk said, "We have paid for our passages, and if they will take us, we shall go willingly, but if not, we shall inquire and look for other means of passage."

"They spoke thus," says Geoffrey, "because they wished that the host should fall to pieces and each return to his own land."

But the finer spirits preferred to face ruin, as far as worldly prospects went, and to go penniless with the host, rather than that the expedition should fail. "For God," said they, "will doubtless repay us when it so pleases Him."

So they began to give and to borrow all that they could. "Then might you have seen many a fine vessel of silver and gold borne in payment to the palace of the Doge." But still a large part of the sum required was lacking.

Then the Doge, seeing their plight, made a proposal to them. To his own citizens he said, "Signors, these people cannot pay more, and in so far as they have paid at all, we have benefited by an agreement that they cannot now fulfil. But our right to keep this money would not everywhere be acknowledged, and if we so kept it, we should be greatly blamed, both us and our land. Let us therefore offer them terms.

"'The King of Hungary has taken from us Zara, in Sclavonia, which is one of the strongest places in the world; and never shall we recover it with all the power that we possess, save with the help of these people. Let us therefore ask them to help us to reconquer it, and we will remit the payment of the rest of the debt, until such time as it shall please God to allow us to gain the moneys by conquest, we and they together.'

"And to this the Venetians and the Crusading host agreed." A striking and pathetic scene followed.

On a very high festival the church of St Mark was thronged with citizens, barons and pilgrims. Before High Mass began, the blind and aged Doge, Henry Dandolo, was led up to the reading-desk, from whence he spoke thus to his people.

"'Signors, you are associated with the most worthy people in the world, and for the highest enterprise ever undertaken; and I am a man, old and feeble, who should have need of rest, and I am sick in body; but I see that no one could command and lead you like myself, who am your lord.

The Fleet of the Fifth Crusade sets sail from Venice

"If you will consent that I take the Sign of the Cross to guard and direct you, and that my son remain in my place to guard the land, then shall I go to live or die with you and with the pilgrims.'

"And when they heard him, they cried with one voice, 'We pray you by God that you consent and do it, and that you come with us!'"

"He was of a great heart," says Geoffrey, comparing him bitterly with those who had gone to other ports to escape danger.

"Then he came down from the reading-desk, and went before the altar, and knelt upon his knees, greatly weeping. And they sewed the cross on to a great cotton hat which he wore, and in front because he wished that all men should see it."

His example sent many of the Venetians to follow in his steps, and at the same time preparations were hurried on for the departure, for September was now nigh at hand.

Just before they started, messengers appeared in their midst with an appeal that was destined to change the whole aim of the Fifth Crusade.

"At that time," says Geoffrey in his terse way, "there was an emperor in Constantinople whose name was Isaac, and he had a brother, Alexios by name, whom he had ransomed from captivity among the Turks. This Alexios took his brother, the Emperor, tore the eyes out of his head, and made himself emperor by the aforesaid treachery. He kept Isaac a long time in prison, together with his son Alexios. This son escaped from prison, and fled in a ship to a city on the sea, which is called Ancona. "Thence he departed to go to King Philip of Germany, who had married his sister, and so came to Verona, in Lombardy, and lodged in the town, and found there a number of pilgrims and other people who were on their way to join the host.

"And those who had helped him to escape, and were with him, said, 'Sire, here is an army in Venice, quite near to us, the best and most valiant people and knights that are in the world, and they are going oversea. Cry to them therefore for mercy, that they have pity on thee and on thy father, who have been so wrongfully dispossessed. And if they be willing to help thee, thou shalt be guided by them. Perchance they will take pity on thy estate.'

"So the young Alexios said he would do this right willingly, and that the advice was good."

Then he sent envoys to the Marquis of Montferrat, chief of the host, and the barons agreed that if he would help them to recover the land oversea, they would help him to recover the land so wrongfully wrested from him and his father. They sent also an envoy with the prince to King Philip of Germany; and in consequence, a goodly number of German soldiers joined the host at Venice and prepared to aid them in their enterprise.

And then, after long delay, the Crusading army set out from the port of Venice in the month of October, 1202.

CHAPTER XIV

The Forsaking of the High Enterprise

'Tis Greece, but living Greece no more.

BYRON: *Childe Harold.*

The Siege of Zara affords one more example of the fatal disunion which was always appearing among the ranks of the Crusaders.

From the first, the Abbot de Vaux, who had to some extent taken the place of the priest Fulk (now gone to his rest), had protested against warring upon the King of Hungary, who was himself a Crusader. The Pope sent urgent messages forbidding the whole enterprise; and when he found that the Venetians paid no heed to this prohibition, the Marquis of Montferrat, leader of the host, found convenient business which would for some time detain him from leading the host against his fellow-Christians.

Even when the Crusaders assembled before the city walls, there were plenty of traitors in the camp only too ready to work mischief. When the people of Zara, utterly dismayed at the sight of the great host before their walls, sent messengers to the Doge, offering to yield up city and goods, if only their lives were spared, the latter replied, quite rightly, that he must first get the consent of the counts and barons of the Crusading pilgrims before he could accept any conditions.

But while the Doge tried to obtain this consent, some of the discontented and disloyal members were busy talking to the envoys. "Why should you surrender your city? The pilgrims will not attack you—have no fear of them. If you can defend yourselves against the Venetians, you will be safe enough." One of them even went upon the walls of the city and made a similar declaration to the citizens.

Consequently the envoys returned to those who sent them, and the negotiations were broken off.

Meantime the Doge and the barons had promptly decided to accept the conditions offered, and were returning to make this known in public, when the Abbot de Vaux confronted the council with— "Lords, I forbid you on the part of the Pope of Rome to attack this city; for those within it are Christians and you are pilgrims," and then informed the Doge that the envoys had departed.

Great was the wrath of Dandolo, as he declared to the counts and barons, "Signors, I had this city, by their own agreement, at my mercy, and your people have broken that agreement; you have covenanted to help me to conquer it, and I summon you to do so."

"Now are we ashamed if we do not help to take the city," was the verdict of the Crusaders when the matter had been discussed, and they came to the Doge and said:

"Sire, we will help you to take the city in despite of those who would let and hinder us."

It was a sorry business altogether, that siege of Zara, and though we may sympathise with their reluctance to attack their fellow-Christians with the arms destined for the fall of Islam, we must remember the solemn undertaking given to the Doge in payment of a just debt. Fortunately the siege lasted but five days, when the citizens, finding their position hopeless, surrendered the city on condition that their lives were spared. With great generosity the Doge divided the town into two parts, and handed one over to the French for winter quarters. The Venetians settled on the other, for it was impossible to return before Easter.

Scarcely had they been lodged there three days when "there began a fray, exceeding fell and fierce, between the Venetians and the Franks ... and the fray was so fierce that there were but few streets in which battle did not rage with swords and lances and cross-bows and darts; and many people were killed and wounded."

Perhaps this incident served to convince the leaders of the difficulty of inducing the quarrelsome soldiers of two nations to sit down together in peace for any considerable period, and to induce them to look with more favour upon their next visitors. These were the envoys of King Philip of Germany and the young Alexios, who came, bringing this message to the Crusaders and the Doge:

"Lords," said King Philip, "I will send you the brother of my wife, and I commit him into the hands of God—may He keep him from death—and into your hands. And because you have fared forth for God, and for right, and for justice, therefore are you bound, in so far as you are able, to restore to their own inheritance those who have been unrighteously despoiled. And my wife's brother will make with you the best terms ever offered to any people, and give you the most puissant help for the recovery of the land oversea."

This proposal was the occasion of much debate. The Abbot de Vaux was all for the dispersal of the host, or an immediate advance upon Palestine. The other side pointed out that they would not be able to do anything, disunited as they were, if they went to Palestine, and that it was only "by way of Babylon or of Greece, that the land oversea could actually be recovered."

"If we reject this covenant," they urged, "we shall be shamed to all time."

So the treaty with Alexios was accepted, even by the Marquis of Montferrat, who had at first held aloof in deference to the wishes of the Pope. Innocent himself did all in his power to break down their resolve, hurling the bolt of excommunication upon the Venetians, and warning the Crusaders that the Empire of Constantinople was under his special protection. But Dandolo remained unmoved, and the Crusading chiefs, influenced by the desire for the rich booty of Constantinople, were all on his side save Simon de Montfort, who betook himself, with his men, and several of his colleagues, forthwith to the Court of Hungary. It was pointed out to the Pope that the fall of Constantinople would bring back the Eastern Church within the fold of the Western Church, and the threats of Innocent grew fainter and fainter as preparation for the attack went on apace, and the young prince Alexios himself joined the host at Zara.

So, on the Eve of Pentecost, 1203, "there were all the ships assembled, and all the transports, and all the galleys of the host, and many other ships of merchants that fared with them. And the day was fine and clear, and the wind soft and favourable, and they unfurled all their sails to the breeze.

"And Geoffrey, the Marshal of Champagne, who dictates this work, *and has never lied therein by one word to his knowledge*, and who was, moreover, present at all the councils held—he bears witness that never was yet seen so fair a sight. Well might it appear that such a fleet would conquer and gain lands, for, far as the eye could reach, there was no space without sails, and ships, and vessels, so that the hearts of men rejoiced greatly."

At the Straits of Malea they met two ships full of the pilgrims who had deserted them at Venice and taken their own way; "Who, when they saw our fleet so rich and well-appointed, conceived such shame that they dared not show themselves."

From one of these a sergeant suddenly let himself down into a boat, saying to those on deck, "I am quits to you for any goods of mine that may remain in the ship, for I am going with these people, for well I deem they will conquer lands."

"Much did we make of the sergeant," comments Geoffrey, quaintly, "and gladly was he received into the host. For well may it be said, that even after following a thousand crooked ways a man may find his way right in the end."

And so at length they came to the port of St Stephen, from whence they had a good view of Constantinople. "Upon which they looked very earnestly, for they never thought there could be in the world so rich a city; and they marked the high walls and strong towers that enclosed it round about, and the rich palaces and mighty churches—of which there were so many that no one would have believed it who had not seen it with his eyes—and the height and length of that city which above all others was sovereign.

"And be it known to you that no man there was of such hardihood, but his flesh trembled; and it was no wonder, for never was so great an enterprise undertaken by any people since the Creation of the World!

"Next day they took port before the magnificent royal palace that faced the city, just across the straits, and finding plenty of corn, for it was harvest time, the leaders took possession of the palace, and all were well content."

It was not long before the usurping Emperor Alexios realised his peril, and sent to them envoys bearing fair messages.

"Lords," said they, "the Emperor Alexios would have you know that he is well aware that you are the best people uncrowned, and come from the best land on earth. And he marvels much why, and for what purpose, you have come into his land and kingdom. For you are Christians, and he is a Christian, and well he knows that you are on your way to deliver the Holy Land oversea and the Holy Cross and the Sepulchre.

"If you are poor and in want, he will right willingly give you of his food and substance, provided you depart out of his land. Neither would he otherwise wish to do you any hurt, though he has full power therein, seeing that if you were twenty times as numerous as you are, you would not be able to get away without utter discomfiture if so be that he wished to harm you."

"Then arose that good knight, Conon of Bethune, and said, 'Fair sirs, you have told us that your lord marvels much why we should have entered into his kingdom and land. Into his land they have not entered, for he holds this land wrongfully and wickedly, against God and against reason. It belongs to his nephew, who sits upon a throne among us, and is the son of his brother, the Emperor Isaac. But, if he is willing to throw himself upon the mercy of his nephew and to give him back his crown and empire, then will we pray his nephew to forgive him, and bestow upon him as much as will enable him to live in wealth. And if you come not as the bearer of such a message, then be not so bold as to come here again.'"

Next morning the Crusaders determined to show the young Alexios to the people of the city; so the Doge of Venice and the Marquis of Montferrat entered into one galley, taking the prince with them, and the knights and barons crowded into as many other boats as they could get. They came close to the city walls and showed the youth to the Greeks, saying, "Behold your natural lord! And be it known to you that I have not come to do you harm, but have come to guard and defend you, if so be that you return to your duty. Now behold the rightful heir. If you hold with him you will be doing as you ought, and if not, we will do to you the very worst that we can."

But the citizens were far too much in awe of the Emperor Alexios to show a sign of sympathy, and so they returned to the host.

Then a terrible siege began, and for ten days both sides fought with might and main. One of the most interesting incidents is thus related by the eye-witness Geoffrey.

"Now may you hear of a strange deed of prowess; for the Doge of Venice, who was an old man and saw naught (seeing he was blind) stood, fully armed, on the prow of his galley, and had the standard of St Mark before him; and he cried to his people to put him on land, or else that he would do justice upon their bodies with his hands.

"And so they did, for the galley was run aground, and they leapt therefrom, and bore the standard of St Mark before him on the land.

"And when the Venetians saw the standard of St Mark on land, and the galley of their lord touching ground before them, each held himself for shamed, and they all got to the land, and those in the transports leapt forth and landed; and those in the big ships got into barges, and made for the shore, each and all as best they could.

"Then might you have seen an assault, great and marvellous and to this bears witness Geoffrey de Villehardouin, who makes this book, that more than forty people told him for sooth that they saw the standard of St Mark of Venice at the top of one of the towers, and that no man knew who bore it thither.

"Now hear of a strange miracle. Those that are within the city fly and abandon the walls, and the Venetians enter in, each as fast and as best he can, and seize twenty-five of the towers, and man them with their own people."

That same night, after a disgraceful retreat from a conflict before the gates, the Emperor Alexios "took of his treasure as much as he could carry, and of his people as many as would go," and fled from the city.

The rest of the citizens drew the poor blind Isaac from his dungeon, clothed him in the imperial robes, and seating him on a high throne, did obeisance to him; after which they hastened to tell the prince Alexios and the barons of what had happened.

Great was the joy throughout the host. "Him whom God will help can no men injure," was said of young Alexios, yet with the distrust which the Greeks always inspired, the leaders hastened to send envoys to enquire whether Isaac meant to ratify the covenant made by the prince, his son. With much reluctance, this was done, though the words with which the request was received might well be thought to ring false.

"Certes," said the Emperor, "this covenant is very onerous, and I do not see how effect can be given to it, nevertheless, you have done us such service, both to my son and to myself, that if we bestowed upon you the whole empire, you would have deserved it well."

There was now nothing else to wait for save the coronation of the new Emperor, and when once that was over, had their hearts been really set upon the cause of God, they would resolutely have turned their faces to the Holy Land. But they had already too lightly forsaken their high enterprise, and readily turned away again from its fulfilment.

CHAPTER XV

The Story of the Latin Empire
of Constantinople

Greece, change thy lords, thy state is still the same,
Thy glorious day is o'er, but not thy years of shame.

BYRON: *Childe Harold.*

Although the usurper had fled, the position of the Emperor Isaac, and that of his son Alexios, the virtual ruler, was by no means serene. Money had to be raised in order to pay the sum promised to the Crusaders, and the taxes levied in consequence did not endear them to the Turks. They had good reason to distrust the loyalty of their subjects, and to dread what might happen if the Crusaders withdrew from the neighbourhood of the city.

So the young prince Alexios, betook himself to the camp and in his father's name used his utmost powers of persuasion to induce the chieftains to remain.

"You have restored to me life, honour and empire," said he "I ought to desire but one thing more, the power to fulfil my promises. But if you abandon me now and proceed to Syria, it is impossible that I should furnish you with either the money, troops or vessels that I have promised. The people of Constantinople have received me with many demonstrations of joy, but they love me not the more for that. I am hated by them because you have restored to me my heritage. If you forsake me, my life or throne would probably fall a sacrifice to my enemies. I implore you, therefore, to defer your departure until the March of next year, and I will promise in return not only to provide your army with all necessary supplies till Easter, but also to engage the Venetians to support you with their fleet till Michaelmas."

The usual division of opinion followed, but the supporters of the Emperor had their way, and the latter showed his gratitude by paying large sums of money to his allies, money that had to be raised by heavy taxes or by selling the treasures stored in the churches. This measure did more than anything else to inflame the Greeks against the Crusaders, for it lent colour to a report that had got about, to the effect that the ancient religion of the Greek Catholics was about to be altered in many ways, and brought into line with that of the Church of Rome.

It was while the young Alexios was absent on a kind of triumphal march through his father's dominions that the suppressed fury of the citizens was kindled into a blaze by the rude behaviour of a handful of the Crusaders.

There was a mosque at Constantinople, which had been built at the request of Saladin for the use of the followers of Islam. From this the worshippers were one day emerging when a band of half intoxicated Flemings and Venetians endeavoured to insult them by forcing an entry. The Mohammedans protected their building with all their energy, and their opponents promptly set it on fire. The fire spread to the neighbouring buildings, and the quarrel, at first a mere street-fight, grew fast and furious.

"No man could put out or abate that fire," says Geoffrey, "it waxed so great and horrible. And when the barons of the host, who were quartered on the other side of the fort, saw this, they were sore grieved and filled with pity—seeing the great churches and the rich palaces melting and falling in, and the great streets filled with merchandise burning in the flames; but they could do nothing."

For two days and two nights the fire lasted, and so strong was the feeling of the city that all Latin settlers there fled with their goods and took refuge in the Crusaders' camp. Again and again the fire broke out, until from east to west its track could be marked out by one unbroken line of destruction and desolation. From the height where their camp was pitched, the Crusaders could but watch the terrible scene with dismay, knowing, as they did, that their men had been its cause.

The return of Alexios did not mend matters. A silence as of death reigned in the blackened streets; looks of hatred met him wherever the people were to be accosted. Moreover, the fact that he had by no means fulfilled his promises of payment to the host led to deep distrust of him in that quarter. Envoys were sent to demand that the Emperor should keep his pledged word, and their speech to him ended with these significant words.

"'Should you do so, it shall be well. If not, be it known to you that from this day forth, they will not hold you as lord or friend, but will endeavour to obtain their due by all the means in their power. And of this they now give you warning, seeing that they would not injure you, nor any one, without first defiance given; for never have they acted treacherously, nor in their land is it customary to do so.'"

There was but one answer to this defiance, seeing that the Emperor could not pay even if he would. He knew too well that he and his son had forfeited even the natural respect due to their position; Isaac, because he was a mere figure-head completely in the hands of Alexios, the real Emperor in all but name; and the latter because of the want of dignity he had shown even in his most friendly days, when on visiting the camp, he had permitted the rough Venetian sailors to snatch off his jewelled circlet and to force upon his head one of the dirty linen caps worn by themselves.

Just at this time, too, the young prince was very much under the influence of a certain "Mourzoufle," or "He of the black eyebrows," as the nickname implies. This man, having laid his own plans in secret, strongly advised Alexios to defy the Crusaders; and so the war began with an unexpected piece of trickery on the part of the Greeks.

"They took seven large ships and filled them full of big logs, and shavings and tow and resin and barrels, and then waited until such time as the wind should blow strongly from their side of the straits. And, one night, at midnight, they set fire to the ships, and unfurled their sails to the wind. And the flames blazed up high, so that it seemed as if the whole world were afire. Thus did the burning ships come towards the fleet of the pilgrims and a great cry arose in the host, and all sprang to arms on every side. It seemed as though every ship in the harbour would fall a victim to this device, but the Venetians did good service on that day, turning the burning boats out of the harbour with such skill that only one ship was utterly destroyed."

From the walls of Constantinople the Greeks had watched what they hoped would be a heavy blow to the Crusaders, who, bereft of their fleet, would not be able to get away either by land or sea. Great was their dismay when they perceived that the main effect was to rouse the pilgrims to take a desperate revenge upon them for their dastardly deeds.

Now came forward the crafty Mourzoufle, and, whilst pretending to act as go-between for Isaac and the French barons, secretly stirred up a revolution in the city against the Emperor.

Just as he had succeeded in convincing Alexios that it was unsafe for him to have anything to do with the Crusaders, a tumult broke out in the city. Crowding into the great church of St Sophia, a reckless mob pronounced that Isaac and Alexios were deposed, and elected an unknown and feeble-minded youth, named Canabus, in their place.

When Alexios heard of this, he shut himself up within the royal palace and sent messengers to Boniface, Marquis of Montferrat imploring his help. But while the Marquis was generously hastening to protect him, Mourzoufle was before him, and was whispering in the ear of the young man that the appearance of Boniface meant that the Latins had seized Constantinople for their own. His allies were busy spreading a report of the assault of the city by the Crusaders, and when Montferrat thundered at the gates of the palace, he was not only refused admittance but found himself in a position of the greatest danger from the fury of the people who thronged the streets.

While he was fighting his way through these, the terrified Alexios had put himself into the hands of Mourzoufle, who promised to lead him to a place of safety. This turned out to be a dungeon, from which the unfortunate young prince was never again to emerge alive.

Regardless of the election of poor wretched Canabus, Mourzoufle now appealed to the people to state their will, saying that until they made this known he was holding captive an Emperor whose plans were not to be trusted. A great shout from the fickle Greeks proclaimed "He of the Black Brows," as their new choice, and he was forthwith carried to St Sophia and crowned as Emperor.

"When the Emperor Isaac heard that his son was taken and Mourzoufle crowned, great fear came upon him, and he fell into a sickness that lasted no long time. So he died. And the Emperor Mourzoufle caused the son, whom he had in prison to be poisoned two or three times; but it did not please God that he should thus die. Afterwards the Emperor went and strangled him, and when he had strangled him, he caused it to be reported everywhere that he had died a natural death, and had him mourned for and buried honourably as an Emperor, and made great show of grief."

"But," as Geoffrey further remarks, "murder cannot be hid, and this deed of the Black-Browed only hastened on the attack which the Crusaders were about to make upon the city."

The aim of this second siege of Constantinople was not merely to punish the murder of the Emperor. The Crusaders had resolved that, from henceforth, no Greek, but a Latin sovereign should rule the Eastern Empire, to be elected by an equal number of French and Venetians acting as a committee.

One of the most interesting incidents of the siege is told us by another chronicler, Robert of Clari. He tells us that a small troop of besiegers had come to a postern door in the city walls which had been newly bricked up. Amongst them was a clerk named Aleaume of Clari, who had done more deeds of prowess than any man in the host, "save only the Lord Peter of Bracuel."

"So when they came to the postern they began to hew and pick at it very hardily; but the bolts flew at them so thick, and so many stones were hurled at them from the wall, that it seemed as if they would be buried beneath the stones. And those who were below held up targets and shields to cover them that were picking and hewing underneath; and those above threw down pots of boiling pitch and fire and large rocks, so that it was one of God's miracles that the assailants were not utterly confounded; for my Lord Peter and his men suffered more than enough of blows and grievous danger. However, so did they hack at the postern that they made a great hole therein, whereupon they all swarmed to the opening, but saw so many people above and below, that it seemed as if half the world were there, and they dared not be so bold as to enter.

"Now when Aleaume, the clerk, saw that no man dared to go in; he sprang forward and said that go in he would. And there was present a knight, a brother to the clerk (his name was Robert), who forbade him and said he should not go in. And the clerk said he would, and scrambled in on his hands and feet. And when the knight saw this he took hold of him by the foot and began to drag him back. But in spite of this, the clerk went in. And when he was within, many of the Greeks ran upon him and those on the wall cast big stones on him; and the clerk drew his knife and ran at them; and he drove them before him as though they had been cattle, and cried to those outside, to the Lord Peter and his folk, 'Sire, come in boldly, I see that they are falling back discomfited and flying.' When my Lord Peter heard this they entered in, and there was with him about ten knights and some sixty foot soldiers, and when those on the wall saw them they fled helter-skelter.

"Now the Emperor Mourzoufle, the traitor, was near by, and he caused the silver horns to be sounded, and the cymbals, and a great noise to be made. And when he saw my Lord Peter and his men, all on foot, he made a great show of falling upon them, and spurring forward, came about half-way to where they stood. But my Lord Peter, when he saw him coming, began to encourage his people and to say, 'Now, Lord God, grant that we may do well, and the battle shall be ours. Let no one dare to think of retreat, but each bethink himself to do well.' Then Mourzoufle, seeing that they would in no wise give way, stayed where he was and then turned back to his tents."

One likes to dwell upon such brave tales as this, that one may the longer defer the miserable sequel of this success.

The city was taken on the Monday of the Holy Week of 1204, when Mourzoufle had shut himself within his palace as a preliminary to flight at the first opportunity.

On the Tuesday, when he had fled from the Golden Gate, the Crusaders occupied the whole city "for they found none to oppose them." The bishops and clergy who were with the host had strictly charged the soldiers to respect the churches of the city, as well as the monks and nuns of the religious houses, but they had spoken in vain.

The taking of the city was disgraced by the most terrible scenes of violence, cruelty, and sacrilege. The beautiful church of St Sophia was defiled by drunken wretches, who drained the sacred vessels from the altar, and sang low songs where only the stately psalms and hymns of the Eastern Church had been heard. Not one sacred building was spared, but rifled of its treasures; its costly lace and beautiful carving was left bare and desolate, too often stained with the blood of the slain. No wonder that the Greeks regarded with utter horror the behaviour of their fellow Christians, who had once been so eager to urge the union of the Churches of East and West. Well might the pope exclaim, when he heard of the horrible excesses, "How shall the Greek Church return to unity and to respect for the Bishop of Rome, when they have seen in the Latins only examples of wickedness and works of darkness, for which they might justly loathe them, worse than dogs?"

Nor were the churches the only objects of the spoilers. Some of the beautiful statues, the work of Greek sculptors in the best days of the art of Greece, were smashed to atoms by the rough soldiers; others, of bronze, were ruthlessly melted down into money.

Many of the inhabitants of the city fled, amongst whom was the Patriarch, or Archbishop, who had scarcely time to clothe himself, and was without food or money. The misery and humiliation of the proud city of Constantine were completed when Baldwin, Count of Flanders, a brave young baron, but utterly out of sympathy with Greek ideas, was crowned Emperor.

The story of the Latin empire of Constantinople scarcely belongs to that of the Crusades. It lasted for fifty-seven years (1204-1261), and was marked by the constant unrest and revolution of one part of the empire or another. Thus it never became firmly settled, for the Latin Emperor had no real power in the land. A short time after his election, most of the Crusaders returned to their own homes.

Two years after the taking of the city, both Boniface of Montferrat, leader of the expedition, and the brave old Dandolo, Doge of Venice, died. The latter may perhaps be blamed as being the means of turning aside the Crusaders from their original undertaking, the relief of the Holy Land; but the real blame lies with those who broke their promise to share in the expenses of the expedition and thus forced the host to do as Dandolo required of them.

What then had become of those faithless remnants of the Fifth Crusade? Their story is soon told.

One small army reached Palestine and strove to join Bohemond of Antioch, a descendant of the famous Crusader. Falling into an ambush of the Saracens, the whole of the force was massacred or taken prisoner, with the exception of a single knight. Another section of the Crusaders actually reached Antioch and became absorbed in the quarrels between Bohemond and the Christian prince of Armenia. Not a blow was struck for the deliverance of Jerusalem, and nothing was gained by the Crusade as far as the Holy War was concerned.

On the other hand, the Fifth Crusade has an importance all its own; for the capture of Constantinople opened a door to the East that had been closed too long. Not only did it sow the seeds of that commercial prosperity which made Venice "hold the gorgeous East in fee, and be the safeguard of the West," but it enabled Western Europe to catch a glimpse of that wealth of art and literature which were stored within the city walls, and which were not to be spread broadcast over the land until the days of her fall into the hands of Islam.

CHAPTER XVI

The Children's Crusade

The child spake nobly: strange to hear
His infantine soft accents clear
Charged with high meanings, did appear.

E. B. BROWNING: *A Vision of Poets.*

During the ten years that followed the taking of Constantinople, Pope Innocent tried to stir up another Crusade, which he hoped should actually fulfil its high ideals.

But the old enthusiasm for the Holy War had died down. The chief kingdoms of Europe were too busy quarrelling with one another to have leisure to think of the distant lands of the East. John of England was getting into trouble both with his own people and with the Pope himself; Philip Augustus of France was building up his kingdom into a great and united nation; Otho of Germany and Frederick II., grandson of Barbarossa, the Crusader, were in fierce conflict with regard to Germany.

While Europe was thus absorbed in more or less selfish aims and ideals, a bitter cry for help was heard from the East. A terrible famine, followed by pestilence, both caused by the failure of the Nile to overflow its banks and fertilize the soil, had reduced the people of Palestine and Egypt to a state of absolute misery. Mothers were said actually to have killed and eaten their own babes in their extremity of hunger, and hundreds of people simply lay down and died by the roadside.

The extreme limit of misery and human desolation was reached when to famine and pestilence was added an earthquake which destroyed whole cities. Heavy, indeed, seemed the hand of God upon His land, and there were not wanting many who said that He was punishing it for past sins and present negligence, since Jerusalem was still in the hands of the infidel.

Suddenly, while Pope Innocent was vainly trying to rouse Europe to undertake a Sixth Crusade, an astonishing movement began to be seen amongst the children of the different lands. Throughout France and Germany boy leaders drilled their little regiments, fastened on the Cross, and prepared seriously to go forth to the Holy War. At first they met with opposition, and ridicule; but such was the earnest zeal of these little people that even the most hardened onlooker ceased to jeer or hinder. Mothers, with aching hearts, saw their little ones march forth, and put out no hand to prevent them, and as the procession passed along the high roads, the children swarmed out from cottage and castle to join the ranks.

From Germany a band of seven thousand children set out for the port of Genoa, from whence they hoped to embark for the Holy Land. They were led by a boy named Nicholas, who swayed them by the most extraordinary power, and was almost worshipped by his little host.

But to get to Genoa, they had to cross the Alps, and there cold and hunger left thousands of the poor mites dead upon the mountain side. The remnant, a sad and sorry spectacle, ragged, starving and dirty, made its way at length into Genoa. There they hoped to find friends and help to cross the sea; but the citizens of the port looked with scant favour upon the little Crusaders, and the Senate ordered that they should forthwith depart from the city. Some wealthy inhabitants, kinder of heart than the rest, adopted a few of the fairer and more attractive children; a few more struggled on to Rome to lay their cause at the feet of the Pope. The rest, heart-sick and weary, tried to struggle back to their homes. Enthusiasm was long since dead, they were laughed at, as failures, and saddest of all, when they were asked why they had left their homes, they now made weary answer that "they could not tell."

Few indeed, ever saw their native land again.

The Children crossing the Alps   197

The Children crossing the Alps

Another band of German boys and girls succeeded in reaching the port of Brindisi, where they were actually put on board ships bound for the East. What was their fate remains a mystery; they were never heard of more.

The largest band of all started from Vendôme in France, under the leadership of a nameless shepherd-boy, who wore a little sheepskin coat and carried a banner upon which was worked a lamb.

He seemed to possess a magic power over his playmates, for at the sound of his clear, high young voice, hundreds and thousands of children flocked to his banner and received the cross from his hands. Not even grown persons, not even the most obstinate parent could stand against his persuasions and entreaties. Full of devotion, full of zeal, the children marched upon the long road to Marseilles, singing psalms and hymns, and crying constantly aloud—

"O Lord Christ! Restore to us thy Cross!"

"You know not what is before you," said the wise greybeards of the villages through which they passed. "What do you mean to do?"

"To get to the Holy Land," was the invariable and undaunted answer.

Weary and hungry, with their ranks much thinned by fatigue and the hardships of the way, the Child Crusade entered Marseilles with gallant hearts. For they fully expected that they would find the sea cleft asunder by a miracle, and a pathway prepared for them to the other side. When they found they were mistaken, some turned their faces homeward; but most stayed to see if by any means they could get boats to take them to the Holy Land. To them came presently two merchants, Hugh Ferrens, and William Beco, or Porcus, who had already discovered how to make a fortune by selling European children as slaves to the Saracens. Approaching the eager little ones with kindly words, they offered to lend them seven ships wherein they might be taken across the sea to their destination.

Joyfully the children agreed and set forth with songs and merry cries, cheered by a vast multitude who watched them from the shore. Of that bright-faced band not one ever reached the Holy Land or returned to Europe to tell the tale. At the end of two days, two of the ships were wrecked in a terrible storm and all on board perished.

The rest escaped this peril, and sailed on to Alexandria and other ports, where the poor little passengers were landed and sold as slaves to the Saracens. Twelve of these are said to have won the martyr's crown, because they preferred to die rather than renounce their faith, a few reached the Christian city of Ptolemais after a time, and told their sad story to the enraged inhabitants, the rest were condemned to a life of slavery among the sons of Islam.

Theirs is a sad story, yet we may find in it the awakening of that spirit of devotion which seemed to have died out in Europe.

Pope Innocent, when he heard of this Crusade, might well say, "These children are a reproach to us for slumbering while they fly to the succour of the Holy Land."

From that time preparations for the Sixth Crusade began in good earnest.

CHAPTER XVII

The Story of the Emperor Frederick and the Sixth Crusade

Pride in their port, defiance in their eye,
I see the lords of human kind pass by.

GOLDSMITH: *The Traveller.*

The story of the Sixth Crusade may be told in two parts, one dealing with failure, the other with success. It was the tardy fruit of Pope Innocent's urgent appeal for another Holy War, a war which he himself would have led, had not death cut short his career.

Curiously enough, the actual leader of the first part of the Sixth Crusade was the king of a country whose people had done their utmost to hinder and prevent the First Crusaders on their march to the Holy Land. Andrew, King of Hungary, sailed in 1216 with a large army to Asia; and with him were the Dukes of Austria and Bavaria. At Acre they were joined by other bands of Crusaders, so that in the next year four kings, of Hungary, Armenia, Cyprus, and John of Brienne, "King of Jerusalem," in name alone, were met together within the city walls.

But these later Crusaders, for the most part, were made of sorry stuff. If Andrew had been a second Geoffrey of Bouillon, he might well have restored the kingdom of Jerusalem. He was, however, half-hearted in the work, and would perhaps never have undertaken it had not his dying father laid upon him a solemn obligation to fulfil his own vow. Famine, too, proved a worse enemy than the Saracens, and the latter, knowing this too well, did not attempt to bring about an engagement.

So the Crusaders at first contented themselves with an advance to the river Jordan, in the waters of which they bathed, and then made a peaceful expedition across the plains of Jericho and by the shores of the Sea of Galilee.

Then the soldiers began to get restive, and to ask for what reason they had come so far from their western homes; so it was suddenly decided to attack the Saracen castle on Mount Tabor.

The story of this attempt only serves to emphasise the weakness and inefficiency of the leaders. The castle was guarded by rocky passes and steep heights, which the Saracens defended with their usual skill and courage. But the Crusaders had actually succeeded in driving them from their posts and in forcing their way to the very gates, when panic, inexplicable but complete, seized hold upon them. They retreated in confusion and shame, undeterred by the reproaches of the Patriarch of Jerusalem, who had accompanied the expedition, bearing with him a fragment of the true Cross. Realising, perhaps, that he was not destined to be a hero, Andrew of Hungary returned home, and his example was followed by many of his fellow-pilgrims.

The hopes of John of Brienne, however, were not quite dashed to the ground, for fresh troops of Crusaders from France, Italy and Germany, arrived at Acre during the spring of 1218, and to these was soon added a little English army under William Longsword, Earl of Salisbury.

The combined forces now determined to strike at the Sultan first through Egypt, and urged thereto by John of Brienne, sailed up the Nile to attack Damietta, one of the strong fortresses which guarded that land. The city seemed impregnable, for it was not only surrounded by three thick walls, but was also protected by a double wall on the side facing the Nile, and by a tower built in the middle of the river, from which was stretched to the ramparts an enormously strong iron chain.

The story of this siege is intermingled with strange legends. A high wooden tower had been built upon two of the Crusaders' ships, from which they hoped to attack the river fortress, but this was quickly set on fire by the Saracens, while the banner of the Holy Cross was seen to drift helplessly down the stream. The terrified onlookers from the banks flung themselves on their knees and implored the help of God at this crisis; upon which it is said that the flames died down, while before the astonished eyes of the Crusaders the banner was seen to wave from the top of the tower in the river.

Much encouraged, they made a fresh attack with such vigour that the enemy threw down their arms and the tower was won.

The legend says that when the chief prisoners were brought into the Christian camp, they asked to be shown the troop of white clothed men bearing shining white swords, the brilliance of whose appearance they declared to have so dazzled their eyes that they could not see to fight longer; and so, says the chronicler of these things, "the Crusaders knew that the Lord Christ had sent His Angels to attack that tower."

While the siege of Damietta itself was still in progress, news arrived of the death of Saphadim, the Sultan, and of the accession of his two sons. The "Sword of Religion," as his Moslem followers called Saphadim, had been a wise as well as a valiant ruler; his successors were weak and incapable. Aghast at the thought of losing their famous seaport, and alarmed at the arrival of many new pilgrims, some hailing from France, others from England, the two young men at length sent messengers with an offer wrung from them, they said, "because the power of God was against them."

They promised, in fact, to give up Jerusalem and the whole of Palestine to the Crusaders if the latter would agree to depart at once from Egypt.

Considering that the freeing of the Holy Land from infidel rule was the only true aim of the Crusaders, we can only be amazed at finding that the offer was rejected.

John of Brienne, "the King of Jerusalem," was eager enough to accept it; so too were the Knights Templars and Hospitallers mindful of their vows. But there was present in the camp a certain Cardinal Pelagius, the papal legate, who claimed, as representative of the Pope, to have the final decision in the matter; and he, fearing probably that the supreme power would fall into the hands of John

John of Brienne attacking the River Tower

of Brienne, supported by the French Crusaders and afterwards by the Knights of the Temple and Hospital, carried the day against the Sultan, and caused the siege of Damietta to be resumed.

Plague had already done its work within the walls, and there remained little for the Crusaders to do. Damietta was theirs, and a sorry triumph it proved.

In spite of the frank opposition of John of Brienne, Pelagius now determined to lead the host to the further conquest of Egypt, and a march on Cairo began. Once more the terrified Sultan offered them the same terms, and once more, being, as Philip of France contemptuously said, "so daft as to prefer a town to a kingdom," they refused to give up Damietta, and pursued their way.

Too late repentance came; for the Nile rose with its usual rapidity, the sluices were opened by the Egyptians, the camp was surrounded by water, and baggage and tents were washed away. The unfortunate Crusaders, caught in a trap, were at the mercy of their foes, and were thankful when the Sultan, in pity, offered to let them go free if they would surrender Damietta. They could but agree, since they knew that it required all the little authority that the young Sultan had at his command to prevent his chieftains condemning the whole host to destruction. As it was, the latter were perishing of famine, and tears flowed down the cheeks of John of Brienne, when led as hostage to the Sultan's tent, as he remembered their distress. With that generosity which marks the whole family of Saladin, the Sultan, when he discovered the cause of his grief, at once sent the starving multitude a large store of food.

Thus in darkness and disgrace ended the first part of the Sixth Crusade, which so far had gained nothing but an ill reputation for the Crusaders who had taken part in it.

The leader of the second part of the Sixth Crusade was made of very different stuff from Andrew of Hungary or John of Brienne. When Frederick II., grandson of the great Barbarossa, had been summoned, some eight years before this time, from the leafy groves of his kingdom of Sicily, to be emperor in place of the rebellious Otho, he had taken the cross and promised to lead an army to the Holy Land at the earliest opportunity.

But Otho did not take his deposition quietly, and during the next few years Frederick had his hands too full in his own dominions to fulfil his vow. After Otho's death, two years later than that of the ambitious and energetic Pope Innocent, the new Pope, Honorius, besought the young Emperor to listen to the bitter cry for help which once more came from across the sea. At that time, however, Frederick was completely absorbed in ambitious schemes for himself and his family.

The Pope's influence was strong, however, and it seemed clear that his friendship was absolutely necessary to Frederick's schemes. The position of the Emperor had never been universally acknowledged in past years, and it was now proposed that Honorius should publicly crown Frederick at St Peter's at Rome. This was done in all good faith and fellowship. "Never did Pope love Emperor as he loved his son Frederick," said Honorius as he parted from him after the coronation, with the promise ringing in his ears that the German army should be ready to start on the Crusade during the following year.

But Frederick still delayed, for he saw little chance of winning the glory he coveted under present conditions in the East. He was not going to send an army thither merely to put John of Brienne back on the throne of Jerusalem. Even the news of the loss of Damietta only served to point the moral that without a huge army, for which time and money were absolutely necessary, supreme success could not be achieved.

Then John of Brienne himself landed in Europe to ask in person for the help that was so long in coming. He brought with him his beautiful daughter, Yolande, and her presence inspired the Pope with new hopes. He now proposed that the Emperor Frederick should marry the maiden and go forth to the Holy War as the heir of John of Brienne. The marriage took place in 1225, more than eleven years after Frederick's vow as a Crusader had first been taken. Almost immediately the Emperor showed his real motive in the marriage by declaring that as John held his royal rights only through his wife, they passed on her death to her daughter, through whom they were now held by her husband, and the Emperor therefore at once proclaimed himself "King of Jerusalem."

Not even then, after the unavailing opposition of John had died away, did Frederick start upon the Crusade. In his beautiful Sicilian kingdom, surrounded by learned Jews, cultivated Saracens, Norman troubadours and Italian poets, he had become too easy-going, too tolerant of all forms of faith or of none, to have any real religious motive to stimulate his actions. He was, indeed, inclined to meet even the Sultan of Egypt himself on terms of the friendliest equality.

But Honorius had been succeeded as Pope by the proud and domineering Gregory IX., to whom this spirit of dallying was loathsome. An imperative letter summoning the Emperor to fulfil his broken vow seemed at first to have some real effect, and in the August of 1227 a large army assembled at Brindisi. There the men were seized by fever, and though Frederick actually set sail with the fleet, it was only to return after three days to the harbour of Otranto, while the host dispersed. The Pope was furious, and, paying no heed to the Emperor's plea of sickness, proceeded to excommunicate, "with bell, book and candle," one whom he said had been nursed, tended, and aided by the Church, only to cheat her with false hopes and trickery.

A pretty quarrel now arose. Frederick appealed to the sovereigns of Europe, declaring that his illness had been real and that "the Christian charity which should hold all things together is dried at its very source."

Meantime he treated the ban of excommunication with contempt.

The Pope replied, in the ensuing Holy Week, by putting every place where Frederick happened to visit under an interdict, and threatening to absolve his subjects from their allegiance if this were disregarded. The Emperor took no notice, but, as though to emphasise the injustice with which he had been treated, pushed on his preparations for the Crusade. Setting out to Brindisi, he was met by papal envoys who forbade him to leave Italy until he had done penance for his offences against the Church. His only answer was to send his own messengers to Rome demanding that the interdict be removed, and meantime he set sail for Acre.

All other Crusaders had gone forth with the blessing of the Pope and the Church; this, the most recent of them all, came as an outcast, with the ban of the Church upon him; and his position was bound to be affected thereby. The greater part of his army feared to serve under him, and he landed with only six hundred knights, "more like a pirate than a great king."

The military orders, the Knights of the Hospital and the Temple also refused to acknowledge him, but the scattered pilgrims, eager for a leader at any price, looked upon him with favour and rallied to his standard.

But upon these broken reeds Frederick had little intention of leaning. From the bigoted narrowness of Templars and Hospitallers he gladly turned to the polished and cultivated Sultan, Malek-Camhel, who was quite prepared to renew friendly terms with one whom he held in much respect. For some time they dealt with trifles, comparing their respective skill in verse-making and in music. Then the Emperor sent Camhel his sword and cuirass, and the latter responded by a present of an elephant, some camels, and a quantity of the rich spices and stuffs of the East.

Becoming aware, at length, that these signs of friendship were the cause of mutterings of discontent in the camps both of Islam and of the Crusaders, they at length agreed upon a truce of ten years on the following conditions. The towns of Joppa, Bethlehem and Nazareth were to be given up to the Christians and the city of Jerusalem, with one important exception.

This was the site of the Temple, where now stood the Mosque of Omar, which was to be left to the Saracens.

So Frederick, with his knights, went up to the Holy City, about the season of Mid-Lent, 1229, and entering the Church of the Holy Sepulchre, took the crown from the High Altar and placed it upon his own head; "but there was no prelate, nor priest, nor clerk, to sing or speak."

He next visited the Mosque of Omar, and showed clearly how little he was moved in all this by love for his own faith. For when the Saracens, respecting his supposed feelings, refrained from sounding the muezzin, or bell that calls to prayer, Frederick stopped the order, saying, "You are wrong to fail in your duty to your religion for my sake. God knows, if you were to come to my country, your feelings would not be treated with such respect."

The terms of this treaty enraged both the Moslems against their Sultan and the Church against the Emperor.

At his entrance into the city, the priests and people fled from the presence of Frederick as though from a leper. The very images of the saints in the churches were draped in black; and the triumphant message of Frederick to Gregory, claiming the gratitude of the Church for the restoration of the Holy City, was received with chilling silence.

Then came the startling news that the Pope had put a large army under the leadership of John of Brienne, now the Emperor's greatest enemy, who was about to capture several of his Italian cities.

Hastening to Acre, and well aware of the hostility of those who considered themselves defrauded of the chance of killing the Saracens, Frederick called a great meeting of pilgrims in the plain outside the city. To them he spoke strongly against the mischief caused by the clergy and the Templars in trying to stir up strife, and ordered all the pilgrims, who had now fulfilled their vows, to sail at once for Europe.

Frederick returned to his western lands in 1229, and though he lived till 1250, he never again saw his kingdom of Jerusalem. He had never been a true Crusader at heart, and had not stayed long enough to establish his eastern domain on any firm foundation; but he had, nevertheless, accomplished within a few months what others had failed to do in as many years, and that without any attempt at bloodshed.

CHAPTER XVIII

The Story of the Seventh Crusade

Now cluttering arms, now raging broils of war,
Can pass the noise of dreadful trumpets' clang.

N. GRIMALD: *The Death of Zoroas*, 1550.

The ten years' truce made by Frederick II. with the Sultan Camhel was by no means scrupulously kept by either side.

The smaller Moslem states did not hesitate to attack the Christian towns whenever they saw an opportunity of so doing, and the Templars, who had been from the first entirely against the terms of the truce, continued to fight against the Sultan until, in a pitched battle, they lost their Grand Master and nearly all their adherents.

This occurrence was seized upon hi Europe as the opportunity to stir up a Seventh Crusade. A leader was soon found in the person of Theobald, Count of Champagne and King of Navarre, a renowned "troubadour" and one of the most skilful minstrels and accomplished knights of his day.

Theobald had begun his career as a rebel to the child-king, Louis IX. of France, and aspired to become the leader of that large number of discontented barons who hoped to obtain their independence of the royal power. But the heart of the rebel was touched by the womanly devotion and courage of the young Queen-mother under these trying circumstances. He became her true and loyal knight, and, in obedience to her desire, assumed the Cross and prepared for a Crusade. All his wealth, all his influence was used for this purpose, and many of the rebellious barons were prevailed upon to follow his example.

Just as Theobald and his company were prepared to start from the town of Lyons, a message arrived from Pope Gregory, urging them to give up their project and return to their homes that they might hold themselves in readiness when he should call in their aid in affairs more pressing than those of the Holy Land. The chief of these was the defence of Constantinople, now ruled by Baldwin, son of John of Brienne, who had implored his aid against the attacks of Greeks and Bulgarians; another, scarcely less important, was the violent quarrel between himself and Frederick.

But the French Crusaders were little in sympathy with the ambitious projects of Gregory. They had taken up the Cross with a definite aim, and remembering what had happened in the days of the Fifth Crusade, they would not be deterred by side issues.

They left Europe torn with fierce political and religious conflicts only to find Syria in the same condition.

The Saracen princes were waging war upon each other as well as upon the Christians, and the unhappy people of both religions had to bear the brunt.

Hearing that the Sultan had already seized Jerusalem, some of the Crusaders determined to revenge themselves by an attack upon the territory round Gaza. In vain Theobald urged them to act together and not to waste their strength; they pushed on until they came to a region shut in by barren sand-hills, where they alighted to rest. Suddenly the silence of the desert was broken by the shrill notes of war-music, and the shouts of the foe. Beset on all sides, a few managed to escape; the rest remained to sell their lives or freedom dearly, and incidentally to weaken the forces of Theobald of Navarre by their loss.

The blow was a crushing one, and Theobald seemed now to lose all heart. A vain attempt was made to negotiate a treaty which both sides would accept. All was in confusion, and during the turmoil Theobald quietly retired from the scene with his men, and went home, confessedly a failure.

The position of the Sultan himself, however, was little less difficult. He was beset by civil strife within his dominions, and when a more dreaded adversary appeared upon the scene he was in no condition to offer effective resistance. The new-comer was

Richard, Earl of Cornwall, a namesake and nephew of Richard Lion-heart, whose name was still a terror to the children of Islam. The reputation of the English Earl as a redoubtable man of war had preceded him, and the Sultan showed great anxiety to come to terms. He offered almost immediately to surrender all prisoners and the Holy Land itself, and to this Richard readily agreed.

For the third and last time the Latin kingdom of Jerusalem was established, and for the next two years it remained in Christian hands. Then, just as Pope Innocent IV. succeeded Gregory IX., came a terrible rumour of a new and more dangerous foe than the Saracens.

"In the year 1240," says Matthew of Paris, "that human joys might not long continue, an immense horde of that detestable race of Satan, the Tartars, burst forth from their mountain regions and making their way through rocks almost impregnable, rushed forth like demons loosed from hell; and over-running the country, covering the face of the earth like locusts, they ravaged the eastern countries with lamentable destruction, spreading fire and slaughter wherever they went."

Descending upon the region of the Caspian lake, they drove out the no less savage shepherd people of that district, and these hurled themselves upon Syria.

"Whatever stood against them was cut off by the sword or dragged into captivity; the military orders were almost exterminated in a single battle; and in the pillage of the city, in the profanation of the Holy Sepulchre, the Latins confess and regret the modesty and discipline of the Turks and Saracens."

Such is the gloomy picture painted by Gibbon of this terrible invasion. Christians and Moslems for the first time fought side by side against the foe they had in common, but they could do nothing. The army left to guard Jerusalem, as well as all the inhabitants, save the old and sick, fled at sight of the savage hordes, who, nevertheless, by a cruel trick obtained their fill of slaughter.

Entering the city they hoisted the Cross and the flags of the Crusaders upon the walls of the Holy City, and rang the bells of the different churches all at once.

The Christians heard, paused in their headlong flight, and seeing the red cross flag streaming from the citadel, cried, "God has had mercy on us and has driven away the barbarians."

Thousands of them at once returned, and directly they had entered their homes, the foemen rushed upon them from secret hiding-places and killed or threw into prison every person they found.

In a great pitched battle fought near Gaza the allied armies of the Moslems and the Christians were almost entirely destroyed. Amongst the prisoners was the Prince of Joppa, who was forthwith led before the walls of his own city, placed upon a cross, and threatened with instant death if he would not command his people to surrender. But this brave man only cried to the men upon the walls, "It is your duty to defend this Christian city, and mine to die for Christ," and so, rather than surrender, he suffered death at the hands of a howling mob.

Nevertheless, Joppa was taken, and every other Christian city; and not until the rulers of Egypt and Syria united with each other as well as with the few Christians left, was there any hope of driving the invaders from the land. But even when this was at length accomplished the Holy City remained in the hands of Islam, and all that the Seventh Crusade had accomplished was entirely swept away.

CHAPTER XIX

The Crusade of St Louis
(The Eighth Crusade)

Some grey crusading knight austere
Who bore St Louis company
And came home hurt to death....

MATTHEW ARNOLD: *A Southern Night.*

A hundred years earlier, the news of the destruction of Jerusalem would have stricken all Europe with horror and roused her to action. It was not so now. That earlier fervour of religion which had sent pilgrims rejoicing to an almost certain death had died away, and had been replaced by a more practical form of faith which found its outlet in a zeal for converting the souls of men, and healing their bodies, rather than in a thirst for the blood of infidels.

In the narrow dirty lanes of cities the inspired monk or eager friar was still to be found; but the followers of St Francis of Assisi or St Dominic were soldiers of the Cross in a more Christ-like, if a less military, spirit than Peter the Hermit or Bernard of Clairvaux, and stirred up the people rather to cleaner and healthier lives than to take arms for the Holy War.

Amongst the sovereigns of Europe at this time, of whom Frederick II. was a fair example, there yet remained one of the old type, one who was filled with the purest zeal for religion mingled with the desire to win glory as became a true knight.

This was Louis IX. of France—the St Louis of the Eighth Crusade—who, if he accomplished nothing towards establishing Christian rule in the Holy Land, yet remains to us in history as an example of the very few who took up the Cross and carried on the war, inspired only by holy and unselfish motives.

"Louis and his fair queen appear, indeed, as brilliant stars, shining through the blackness of a sky overcast with clouds; but they could not dispel the darkness, or lend more than a transitory gleam of brightness to illumine the gloomy prospects.

King Louis found a devoted hero-worshipper and chronicler in the Sire de Joinville, a great French noble, who accompanied him upon the Eighth Crusade, and whose story will often be told here in his own words.

Louis IX. came to the French throne at no easy time, for he was but a boy of ten, and the powerful French barons were eager to win their independence of the royal power. But they found their match in the Queen Regent, Blanche of Castile, who, for the first time, put her dependence upon the people of her land, and trusted to them to defend their young king against the rebellion of the nobles. She also, as we have seen, won over to her side Count Theobald of Champagne, by whose help the rebels were soon forced to yield, and who, for love of her, afterwards became one of the leaders in the Seventh Crusade.

The young Louis was brought up by her more as a monk than a king, and, as he grew older, his own tastes turned entirely in the same direction. "You are not a king of France," cried a woman who was trying to win his favour in an unjust cause, "you are a king only of priests and monks. It is a pity that you are king of France. You ought to be turned out."

"You speak truly," was the gentle answer, "it has pleased God to make me king; it had been well had He chosen some one better able to govern this kingdom rightly."

Yet he was one of France's wisest rulers, taking a personal interest in the troubles of her people that was rare, indeed, in those days.

"Ofttimes it happened that he would go, after his mass, and seat himself in the wood of Vincennes, and lean against an oak, and make us sit round him. And all those who had any cause in hand came and spoke to him, without hindrance of usher or any other person. Then would he ask, out of his own mouth, 'Is there anyone who has a cause in hand?' And those who had a cause stood up.

Then would he say, 'Keep silence all and you shall be heard in turn, one after the other.' And when he saw that there was anything to amend in the words of those who spoke on their own behalf, or on behalf of any other person, he would himself, out of his own mouth, amend what he had said."

His love of justice is seen in his answer to the Pope, when Gregory, after a second violent quarrel with the Emperor Frederick, had deposed him and offered the crown to Louis' brother. Gentle as was the King's usual speech, he replies now, "Whence is this pride and daring of the Pope, who thus disinherits a king who has no superior nor even an equal among Christians—a king not convicted of the crimes laid to his charge? To us he has not only appeared innocent, but a good neighbour; we see no cause for suspicion either of his worldly loyalty or of his Catholic faith. This we know, that he has fought valiantly for our Lord Christ both by sea and land. So much religion we have not found in the Pope, who endeavoured to confound and wickedly supplant him in his absence, while he was engaged in the cause of God."

There can be no doubt that it was in his character as a Crusader that Frederick mainly attracted Louis, for he had little else in common with him. For a long time the French King nursed in secret his desire to follow his hero's example, since his mother would not hear of his deserting his own kingdom. But at length the clear call came.

"It happened, as God so willed, that a very grievous sickness came upon the king in Paris, and brought him to such extremity that one of the ladies who was tending him wished to draw the cloth over his face, saying he was dead; but another lady, who was on the other side of the bed, would not suffer it, saying that the soul was still in his body. And as he listened to the debate between these two ladies, Our Lord wrought within him and soon sent him health, for before that he had been dumb and could not speak.

"And as soon as he could speak, he asked that they should give him the Cross, and they did so.

"When the queen, his mother, heard that speech had come back to him, she made as great joy thereof as ever she could. But when she knew that he had taken the Cross—as also he himself told her—she made as great mourning as if she had seen him dead."

Not even his mother's grief could hinder this ardent soldier of the Cross, whose chief wish now was to persuade his nobles to follow him. At the Christmas of that year he presented each of his barons with a new robe. When these were put on, they were found to have the red cross embroidered between the shoulders. The wearers had "taken the cross," and must accompany their king.

Two years were spent in preparing supplies, and at the end of the year 1248, King Louis, with the Queen, his wife, embarked and sailed to Cyprus, where he remained until the spring of 1249. On landing in Egypt at the Point of Limesol, he met with a strange occurrence.

"The king," says Joinville, "landed on the day of Pentecost. After we had heard mass, a fierce and powerful wind, coming from the Egyptian side, arose in such sort, that out of two thousand eight hundred knights, whom the king was taking into Egypt, there remained no more than seven hundred whom the wind had not separated from the king's company, and carried away to Acre and other strange lands, nor did they afterwards return to the king of a long while."

This sounds like a story from the "Arabian Nights," and one can understand the King's haste to escape, with the remnant left him, from the region of this mysterious wind of the desert. So he sailed to Damietta, "and we found there, arrayed on the seashore, all the power of the Sultan—a host fair to look upon, for the Sultan's arms are of gold, and when the sun struck upon them they were resplendent. The noise they made with their cymbals and horns was fearful to listen to."

Waiting only until he saw his ensign of St Denis safe on shore, "the king went across his ship with large steps, and would not leave from following the ensign, but leapt into the sea, which was up to his arm-pits. So he went, with his shield hung to his neck, and his helmet on his head, and his lance in his hand, till he came to his people who were on the shore."

The Landing of St Louis in Egypt   223

The Landing of St Louis in Egypt

Seized with panic at the sight of the many brave ships and the landing of the Crusaders, the garrison of Damietta fled without striking a blow. Says Joinville, "The Saracens sent thrice to the Sultan, by carrier-pigeons, to say that the king had landed, but never received any message in return, because the Sultan's sickness was upon him. Wherefore they thought that the Sultan was dead, and abandoned Damietta.

"Then the king sent for all the prelates of the host, and all chanted with a loud voice, *Te Deum laudamus*.

"Afterwards the king mounted his horse, and we all likewise, and we went and encamped before Damietta."

There they remained until they were joined by the King's brother, the Count of Poitiers; and after that a march was made upon Babylon, "because, if you wanted to kill the serpent, you must first crush its head."

Now when they tried to cross the delta of the Nile, which at that part of Egypt lies between four "branches" of the river, they encamped between the stream that flows to Damietta, and that which flows to Tanis, and found the whole host of the Sultan lying upon the farther side of the latter, and ready to defend the passages.

The King at once gave orders to build a causeway across the river; but as fast as this was made the Saracens dug holes and let in the water which had been dammed up, thus washing away the work. They constantly harassed the camp also, and tried to cut off the French army in the rear; and when they began to use Greek fire also, the hearts of the Crusaders began somewhat to quail.

"The fashion of the Greek fire was such that it came frontwise as large as a bottle of verjuice, and the tail of fire that issued from it, was as large as a large lance. The noise it made in coming was like Heaven's own thunder. It had the seeming of a dragon flying through the air. It gave so great a light because of the great abundance of fire making the light, that one saw as clearly through the camp as if it had been day....

"When my Lord Walter, the good knight who was with me, saw this, he spoke thus: 'Lord, we are in the greatest peril that we have ever been in, for if they set fire to our towers and we remain here, we are but lost and burnt up; while if we leave these defences which we have been sent to guard, we are dishonoured. Wherefore none can defend us in this peril save God alone. So my advice and counsel is, that every time they hurl the fire at us, we throw ourselves on our elbows and knees, and pray to our Saviour to keep us in this peril....'

"Every time that our saintly king heard them hurling the Greek fire, he would raise himself in his bed, and lift up his hands to Our Saviour, and say, weeping, 'Fair Lord God, guard me my people.'

"And verily I believe that his prayers did us good service in our need. At night, every time the fire had fallen, he sent one of his chamberlains to ask how we fared, and whether the fire had done us any hurt."

At length, when things were getting very serious for the Crusading army, there came a Bedouin, or Arab of the desert, to the camp, and offered to show them a ford over the river if they would pay him five hundred besants.

Risky as was the undertaking—for the offer might have been a mere piece of treachery, with the object of placing the host in an entirely unprotected position, and of drowning most of their number—the King decided in its favour, and determined to lead the way, with his three brothers, across the ford.

"Then, as the dawn of day was appearing, we collected from all points and came to the Bedouin's ford; and when we were ready we went to the stream and our horses began to swim. When we got to the middle of the stream, we touched ground and our horses found footing; and on the other bank of the stream were full three hundred Saracens, all mounted on their horses.

"Then said I (the Sire de Joinville) to my people, 'Sirs, look only to the left hand, and let each draw thither; the banks are wet and soft, and the horses are falling upon their riders and drowning them.' Thereupon we moved in such sort that we turned up the stream and found a dry way, and so passed over, thank God! that not one of us fell; and as soon as we had passed over, the Turks fled."

But disaster was at hand. The Templars had been given the post of honour in the vanguard, and close after them came the Count of Artois, brother to the King, with his men.

"Now it so happened that as soon as the Count of Artois had passed over the stream, he and all his people fell upon the Turks, who had fled before them. The Templars notified to him that he was doing them great despite in that, while his place was to come after them, he was going before them, and they besought him to suffer them to go before, as had been arranged by the king. Now it chanced that the Count of Artois did not venture to answer them because of my Lord Foucaud of Merle, who held the bridle of his horse; and this Foucaud of Merle was a very good knight, but heard naught of what the Templars were saying to the Count, seeing that he was deaf, and was all the while crying, 'Out on them! Out on them!'

"Now when the Templars saw this, they thought they would be shamed if they suffered the Count to outride them, so they struck spurs into their horses, helter-skelter, and chased the Turks, and the Turks fled before them, right through the town of Mansourah and into the fields beyond towards Babylon.

"But when the Crusaders thought to return, the Turks threw beams and blocks of wood upon them in the streets, which were narrow. There were killed the Count of Artois, the Lord of Couci, who was called Raoul, and so many other knights that the number was reckoned at three hundred. The Temple, as the Master has since told me, lost there fourteen score men-at-arms, and all mounted."

The whole blame of this disastrous affair must be laid at the door of the Count of Artois, in spite of Joinville's attempt to put it on the shoulders of Lord Foucaud. When the Grand Master of the Templars had warned the Count of the risk of pursuing men who had but given way to a moment's panic, the latter openly accused him of treachery.

"Do you suppose," cried the Master, "that we have left our homes and our substance and taken the habit of a religious in a strange land, only to betray the Cause of God and to forfeit our salvation?"

And with that he prepared to go to almost certain death. Then William Longsword, son of the Earl of Salisbury, did his best to turn the Count from such a course of destruction, and was met with insult. "See how timid are these tailed English! It would be well if the army were purged of such folk!" "At least," returned Longsword, "we English to-day will be where you will not dare to touch our horses' tails."

Longsword fell that day with his face to the foe, Artois, in trying to escape, and the whole force must have been destroyed had not the King's division come to the rescue, while Joinville, who tells the tale, managed to hold the bridge across to the town. Says the latter, "We were all covered with the darts that failed to hit the sergeants. Now it chanced that I found a Saracen's quilted tunic lined with tow: I turned the open side towards me and made a shield of it, which did me good service, for I was only wounded by their darts in five places, and my horse in fifteen. And it chanced again that one of my burgesses of Joinville brought me a pennon with my arms and a lance head thereto, and every time that we saw that the Turks pressed too hardly upon the sergeants, we charged them and they went flying.

"The good Count of Soissons, in that point of danger, jested with me, and said, 'Seneschal, let these curs howl! We shall talk of this day yet, you and I, in ladies' chambers.'"

At sunset, when the King's crossbow men came up, the Saracens fled, and Joinville, hastening to Louis, conducted him with loving care to his tent. "And as we were going, I made him take off his helmet, and lent him my steel cap, so that he might have air.

"When he had passed over the river, there came to him Brother Henry, Provost of the Hospitallers, and kissed his mailed hand. The king asked if he had any tidings of the Count of Artois, his brother, and the Provost said that he had news of him indeed, for he knew of a certainty that his brother, the Count of Artois, was in Paradise.

"'Ah, sire,' said the Provost, 'be of good comfort therein, for never did King of France gain such honour as you have gained this day. For, in order to fight your enemies, you have passed swimmingly over a river, and you have discomfited them, and driven them from the field, and taken their war-engines and also their tents, wherein you will sleep this night.'

"Then the king replied, 'Let God be worshipped for all He has given me!' but the big tears fell from his eyes."

In spite of the Provost's cheering words, the King's army was still in a position of great danger. That very night an attack was made upon the camp, which was but the first of a series of attacks which cut Louis off entirely from Damietta and forced him to retreat to the "Island."

"When I was laid in my bed," says Joinville, "when indeed I had good need of rest because of the wounds received the day before—no rest was vouchsafed to me. For before it was well day, a cry went through the camp, 'To arms! To arms!' I roused my chamberlain, who lay at my feet, and told him to go and see what was the matter. He came back in terror, and said, 'Up, lord, up: for here are the Saracens, who have come on foot and mounted, and discomfited the king's sergeants who kept guard over the engines, and have driven them among the ropes of our tents.'

"I got up and threw a tunic over my back and a steel cap on my head, and cried to our sergeants, 'By St Nicholas, they shall not stay here!' My knights came to me, all wounded as they were, and we drove the Saracens from among the engines, and back towards a great body of mounted Turks."

A day or two later, the Saracens, encouraged by the sight of the bloodstained coat of arms belonging to the Count of Artois, which they were told was that of the King, and that Louis was now dead, came together in a great battle against the French host. In this fight so many on both sides were killed that the river was full of the dead.

The Last Fight of William Longsword   231

The Last Fight of William Longsword

Then a worse thing fell upon them, for, says Joinville, "because of the unhealthiness of the land—where it never rains a drop of water—there came upon us the sickness of the host, which sickness was such that the flesh of our legs dried up and the skin became spotted, black and earth colour, like an old boot; nor could anyone escape from this sickness without death."

Famine followed, for the Turks had cut off all sources of supplies from Damietta; and, in desperation, an attempt to treat with the enemy was made. The conditions proposed were that Louis should give up Damietta in return for the kingdom of Jerusalem; and when the Saracens asked what pledge they offered that they should regain the port, the French offered them one of the King's brothers.

They promptly replied that they would be satisfied with no one but the King himself, whereupon, "my Lord Geoffrey of Sargines, the good knight, said he would rather that the Saracens should have them all dead or captive than bear the reproach of having left the king in pledge."

When Louis saw that there was no alternative but death or retreat, since none of his officers would agree that he should be given up, he once more gave the order to try to return to Damietta. The King could have easily escaped thither by means of a little boat, but he would not abandon his people, many of whom were very sorely sick. But Louis himself was weak with illness, so that he could scarcely sit upon his horse; yet he persisted in trying to guard the river banks while Joinville and others got the sick men on board. What happened then was told by Louis himself to his faithful friend. "He told me that of all his knights and sergeants there only remained behind with him my Lord Geoffrey of Sargines, who brought him to a little village, and there the king was taken. And, as the king related to me, my Lord Geoffrey defended him from the Saracens as a good servitor defends his lord's drinking-cup from flies; for every time that the Saracens approached, he took his spear, which he had placed between himself and the bow of his saddle, and put it to his shoulder and ran upon them, and drove them away from the king. And then they brought the king to the little village; and they lifted him into a house, and laid him, almost as one dead, in the lap of a burgher-woman of Paris, and thought he would not live till night."

Thus did Louis fall into the hands of the Saracens, and was left in sorry plight indeed. He was sufficiently conscious to beg Lord Philip de Montfort to try once again to make terms of peace, but while this was being done, "a very great mischance happened to our people. A traitor sergeant, whose name was Marcel, began to cry to our people, 'Yield, lord knights, for the king commands you; and do not cause the king to be slain!'

"All thought that the king had so commanded, and gave up their swords to the Saracens. The Emir (the officer of the Sultan), saw that the Saracens were bringing in our people prisoners, so he said to my Lord Philip that it was not fitting that he should grant a truce, for he saw very well that we were already fallen into his hands."

Meantime Joinville and his men had fared no better by water than his comrades had by land. He himself, indeed, had the narrowest possible escape from death, and was only saved by the generosity of a Saracen, whose former dealings with Frederick II. of Germany had made him favour the Crusaders. Joinville was exceedingly weak and ill, but as his boat was in mid-stream he hoped to escape to Damietta with those of the sick whom he had been able to rescue.

"My people," says he, "had put on me a jousting hauberk, so that I might not be wounded by the darts that fell into our boat. At this moment my people, who were at the hinder point of the boat, cried out to me, 'Lord, Lord, your mariners, because the Saracens are threatening them, mean to take you to the bank!' Then I had myself raised by the arms, all weak as I was, and drew my sword on them, and told them I should kill them if they took me to the bank. They answered that I must choose which I would have; whether to be taken to the bank, or anchored in mid-stream till the wind fell. I told them I liked better that they should anchor than that they should take me to the shore where there was nothing before us save death. So they anchored.

"Very shortly after we saw four of the Sultan's galleys coming to us, and in them full a thousand men. Then I called together my knights and my people, and asked them which they would rather do, yield to the Sultan's galleys or to those on land. We all agreed that we would rather yield to the galleys, because so we should be kept together, than to those on land, who would separate us and sell us to the Bedouins.

"Then one of my cellarers said, 'Lord, I do not agree in this decision.' I asked him to what he did agree, and he said to me, 'I advise that we should all suffer ourselves to be slain, for then we shall go to Paradise.' But we heeded him not."

When Joinville saw that he must be taken either way, he threw his casket of jewels into the river, and turned to find one of his mariners urging, "Lord, if you do not suffer me to say you are the king's cousin they will kill you all, and us also." So he told him he could say what he pleased. The sailor at once cried out loud, "Alas, that the king's cousin should be taken!" with the result that the Saracens on the nearest galley at once anchored near their boat.

But help of an unexpected kind was at hand. A Saracen, who had lived on land in the East belonging to the Emperor Frederick, swam aboard, and throwing his arms round Joinville's waist, said, "Lord, if you do not take good heed you are but lost; for it behoves you to leap from your vessel on to the bank that rises from the keel of that galley; and if you leap, these people will not mind you, for they are thinking only of the booty to be found in your vessel."

So he leapt, but so weak was he that he tottered and would have fallen into the water had not the Saracen sprung after him and held him up in his arms.

A rough reception awaited him, however, for they threw him on the ground and would have killed him had not the Saracen held him fast in his arms, crying "Cousin to the King!"

He was certainly in sorry case, for he had no clothing save for the steel hauberk, which the Saracen knights, pitying his condition, exchanged for a fur-lined coverlet and a white belt, in which he girt himself for lack of proper clothes. Still under the protection of "his Saracen," Joinville saw with sad eyes the slaughter of the sick upon the bank and in the boats, and was himself subjected to a sore trial of faith. For his protector, who was evidently a man of some authority, tried to tempt him to embrace the religion of Islam by causing all his mariners to be brought before him, telling him that they had all denied their faith.

"But I told him never to place confidence in them, for lightly as they had left us, so lightly, if time and opportunity occurred, would they leave their new masters. And he answered that he agreed with me; for that Saladin was wont to say that never did one see a bad Christian become a good Saracen, or a bad Saracen become a good Christian.

"After these things he caused me to be mounted on a palfrey and to ride by his side. And we passed over a bridge of boats and went to Mansourah, where the King and his people were prisoners. And we came to the entrance of a great pavilion, where the Sultan's scribes were; and there they wrote down my name. Then my Saracen said to me, 'Lord, I shall not follow you further, for I cannot; but I pray you, lord, always to keep hold of the hand of the child you have with you, lest the Saracens should take him from you.'"

Truly, in his case, for the sick and sorry Joinville, as well as for the protection he provided for the little lad, the "child called Bartholomew," that unknown Saracen showed himself worthier of the name of Christian than many of those who fought under the banner of the Cross.

When the French lord entered the pavilion with his little charge, he found it full of his brother barons, "who made such joy that we could not hear one another speak, for they thought they had lost me."

Joy was soon turned to grief, however, for many of their number were taken by the Saracens into an adjoining courtyard and asked, "Wilt thou abjure thy faith?"

"Those who would not abjure were set to one side, and their heads were cut off, and those who abjured were set on the other side."

Then the Sultan sent to ask what terms they were willing to make. "Would you give, for your deliverance, any of the castles belonging to the barons oversea?" But they replied that they had no power over these castles, which belonged to their sovereign King.

Then he asked if they would surrender any of the castles belonging to the Knights Templars and Hospitallers. But they answered that this could not be, for when the knights of the Temple or the Hospital were appointed to these castles, they were made to swear, on holy relics, that they would not surrender any of them for man's deliverance.

"The council of the Sultan then replied that it seemed to them that we had no mind to be delivered, and that they would go and send us such as would make sport of us with their swords, as they had done of the others belonging to our host. And they went their way."

With Louis himself the counsellors of the Sultan had gone still further, threatening him with torture if he did not do as they willed. "To their threats the King replied that he was their prisoner, and that they could do with him according to their will."

Finding that they could not terrorise the King they came back to him once more and asked how much money he was willing to pay for a ransom, besides giving up Damietta.

To this Louis replied that if the Sultan would accept a reasonable sum, he would see if the Queen would pay it for their deliverance. This answer, to those who held the Eastern idea of women, was astounding, and they asked, "How is it that you will not tell us definitely that these things shall be done?" To which Louis replied, with spirit that he did not know if the Queen would consent, seeing that she was his lady, and mistress of her own actions. Then they took counsel with the Sultan, and brought back word that if the Queen would pay five hundred thousand *livres* (about £405,000) he would release the King.

"And when they had taken the oath that this should be so, the King promised that he would willingly pay the five hundred thousand *livres* for the release of his people, and surrender Damietta for the release of his own person, seeing that it was not fitting that such as he should barter himself for coin."

When the Sultan heard this, he said. "By my faith, this Frank is large-hearted not to have bargained over so great a sum! Now go and tell him that I give him a hundred thousand *livres* towards the payment of the ransom."

The prospects of the unfortunate Crusaders seemed therefore to be brightening, when, as they were being conveyed down the river to the Sultan's camp as a preliminary to being set free, all was suddenly darkened again by the murder of their generous captor at the hands of some of his own traitorous Emirs.

One of these, indeed, came to King Louis, with the heart of the Sultan, all reeking with blood, in his hand, and said: "What wilt thou give me? For I have slain thine enemy, who, had he lived, would have slain thee!"

"But the King answered him never a word."

Nothing now but death seemed the probable fate of the despairing prisoners, who meantime, were thrown into the hold of the galley and "so pressed together that my feet came against the good Count Peter of Brittany, and his came against my face."

But the Saracen Emirs seem to have thought that more profit could be made out of them alive than dead, and were ready to observe the terms already proposed, if the King would renew his oath to this effect, "that if he did not observe his covenant he should be as dishonoured as a Christian who denies God and His law, and who spits upon the Cross and tramples on it."

Though he fully meant to keep his word, the pious soul of Saint Louis revolted against so blasphemous a declaration, and he absolutely refused to take such an oath. They threatened him with instant death, but he replied tranquilly that he "liked better to die as a good Christian rather than to live under the wrath of God."

By the exercise of further fiendish cruelty the Saracens attained their object. They took the old white haired Patriarch of Jerusalem, and tied him to the pole of the pavilion with his hands behind his back, and so tightly "that the said hands swelled to the size of his head, and that the blood started from between the nails." Then the Patriarch cried to the King, "Sire, for the love of God, swear without fear; for seeing that you intend to hold to your oath, I take upon my own soul whatsoever there may be of sin in the oath that you take."

It seems certain that by his firmness and courage Louis had earned the respect and admiration of the Saracens. Joinville says that they wanted to make him their Sultan, and only desisted because they said he was the most steadfast Christian that could be found. "They said that if Mohammed had suffered them to be so maltreated as the King had been, they would never have retained their belief in him; and they said further that if their people made the King to be Sultan, they would have to become Christians, or else he would put them all to death."

In spite of this, however, their fate still hung in the balance, for some recalled the precept of Mohammed, "For the assurance of the faith, slay the enemy of the law."

But better counsels prevailed, and on the day after Ascension Day, in the year 1250, all were released save the Count of Poitiers, who remained as hostage till the ransom should be paid.

Many of the Crusading barons no sooner regained their ships than they set sail for France, but the King remained behind, to see that the ransom was paid. In connection with this ransom Joinville tells us of an incident that marks even more emphatically Louis' upright character.

"When the money had been counted, there were those of the council who thought that the King should not hand it over until he had received his brother back. But the King replied that he would hand it over, seeing that he had agreed with the Saracens to do so, and as for the Saracens, if they wished to deal honestly, they would also hold to the terms of their agreement. Then Lord Philip of Nemours told the King that they had miscounted, by ten thousand *livres*, to the loss of the Saracens (but without their knowledge).

"At this the King was very wroth, and said it was his will that the ten thousand *livres* should be restored, seeing he had agreed to pay two hundred thousand before he left the river.

"Then I touched Lord Philip with my foot, and told the King not to believe him, seeing that the Saracens were the wiliest reckoners in the whole world. And Lord Philip said I was saying sooth, for he had only spoken in jest, and the King said such jests were unseemly and untoward. 'And I command you,' said the King to him 'by the fealty that you owe me as being my liegeman—which you are—that if these ten thousand *livres* have not been paid, you will cause them to be paid without fail.'"

Nor would Louis listen to those who advised him to leave the river on account of its proximity to the Saracens, and go to his ship, which waited for him out at sea. But he had promised his foes not to go away until the payment had been made, and no considerations of personal safety would induce him to break his word.

"So soon, however, as the ransom was paid, the King, without being urged thereto, said that henceforth he was acquitted of his oaths, and that we should depart thence, and go to the ship that was on the sea. Then our galley was set in motion, and we went a full great league before we spoke to one another, because of the distress in which we were at leaving the Count of Poitiers In captivity.

"Then came Lord Philip of Montfort in a galleon, and cried to the King: 'Sire! Sire! Speak to your brother, the Count of Poitiers, who is on this other ship!' Then cried the King 'Light up! Light up!' and they did so. Then was there such rejoicing among us that greater could not be. The King went to the Count's ship, and we went too. A poor fisherman went and told the Countess of Poitiers that he had seen the Count released, and she caused twenty *livres* to be given to him."

Nor was Louis the only star to shine in the dark firmament of the Eighth Crusade. All those anxious weeks there lay at Damietta the poor young Queen, in terrible anxiety for the fate of her husband, and for the future of those who were with her in the city.

In the midst of her grief and trouble was born her little son Tristan, the "child of sorrow," and he was but a day old when she heard that all the men of the five cities of Italy, who were with her in the city, were minded to flee away. With heroic courage she sent for them to her bedside and urged them not to leave Damietta to its fate, for if so the King would be utterly lost.

To this they replied: "Lady what can we do? For we are dying of hunger in this city?" But she told them that for famine they need not depart, "for," said she "I will cause all the food in this city to be bought, and will keep you all from henceforth at the King's charges."

Thus did the brave Queen keep Damietta until it had to be given up according to the terms of the treaty; upon which she went to Acre, there to await the King.

The release of the prisoners was, for all practical purposes, the end of the ill-fated Eighth Crusade, but Louis could not bear to return to France without even a glimpse of the Holy Land which lay so very near his heart.

His brother had deserted him, but the faithful Joinville was still at his side, and with the latter was now to be found the little child, Bartholomew, who had in so strange a manner been placed under his protection. There were not wanting those who urged the King to return to France, and look after the affairs of his kingdom, but Louis was firm. The Queen Mother, Blanche, was well able to fill his place, and he was determined not to leave the kingdom of Jerusalem while any hope remained of striking a blow on its behalf. Again and again he had urged Henry III. of England to bring an army to its relief, he had even promised to give up Normandy if he would do this; and he could scarcely believe that he would persist in his refusal. If he should fail there was yet a faint hope that the Pope himself might lead an army in the cause of God; while there was the slightest chance, therefore, he would hold himself ready to act.

So Louis went first to Acre to rejoin his Queen, and then set to work to rebuild the fortifications of the seaports, Cæsarea, Joppa, and Sidon, which had been destroyed by the Saracens, though they were still ruled by Christian chieftains. And then four more years passed away.

It was while Louis was engaged in fortifying Joppa that he was told that the Sultan was willing that he should go to Jerusalem under a "sure and safe conduct." It was the King's dearest wish to visit the Holy Sepulchre, but after grave consideration, acting on the advice of his council, he determined not to do so. His reason was the same as that of Richard of England in the Third Crusade. "For if he, the greatest Christian King, went a pilgrimage without delivering the city from God's enemies, then would all other kings and pilgrims, coming thereafter, rest content with going on pilgrimage after the same manner as the King of France, and give no heed to the deliverance of Jerusalem."

A pilgrimage in sackcloth to Nazareth was all, therefore, that the king would allow himself, and meantime his hopes of aid from Europe grew fainter and fainter.

Then came bad news from France. Queen Blanche, who seems to have been more to the king than wife or children, was dead, and Louis must return to his deserted kingdom. On St Mark's day (April 24th) of the year 1254, the king and queen sailed from Acre, but they were not destined to reach France without further adventures.

"On the Saturday we came in sight of the Isle of Cyprus, and of a mountain in Cyprus which is called the Mountain of the Cross. That Saturday a mist rose from the land, and descended from the land to the sea; and by this our mariners thought we were further from the Isle of Cyprus than we were, because they did not see the mountain above the mist. Wherefore they sailed forward freely and so it happened that our ship struck a reef of sand below the water; and if we had not found that little sandbank where we struck, we should have struck against a great mass of sunken rocks, where our ship would have been broken in pieces, and we all shipwrecked and drowned.

"As soon as our ship struck, a great cry rose in the ship, for each one cried 'Alas!' and the mariners and the rest wrung their hands because each was in fear of drowning.

"When I heard this, I rose from my bed where I was lying, and went to the ship's castle with the mariners. As I came there,

Brother Raymond, who was a Templar and master of the mariners, said to one of his varlets: 'Throw down the lead.' And he did so. And as soon as he had thrown it, he cried out and said. 'Alas, we are aground!' When Brother Raymond heard that, he rent his clothes to the belt, and took to tearing out his beard, and to crying: 'Ay me! Ay me!'"

In marked contrast to this not very helpful master of mariners stands one of Joinville's knights who "brought me, without a word, a lined overcoat of mine, and threw it on my back, for I had donned my tunic only. And I cried out to him, and said, 'what do I want with your overcoat that you bring me, when we are drowning?' And he said to me, 'By my soul, lord, I should like better to see us all drowned than that you should take some sickness from the cold, and so come to your death.'"

An effort was made to get the king off the threatened ship by means of the galleys, but the latter held off; and in this they acted wisely, seeing there were full eight hundred persons on board the ship who would have jumped into the galleys to save their lives, and thus have caused the latter to sink.

Morning came and found the ship fast aground, and seeing there was much damage done to her keel, the servants of the king implored him to embark in another vessel. By his decision Louis showed once again that wonderful unselfishness which forms one of his best claims to the title of Saint.

After hearing the opinion of the master mariners, and his nobles, he called together the seamen and said to them.

"I ask you, on your fealty, whether, if the ship were your own, and freighted with your own merchandise, you would leave her?"

And they replied all together "No!" for they liked better to put their bodies in peril of drowning than to buy a new ship at great cost.

"Why then," asked the king, "do you advise me to leave the ship?"

"Because," said they, "the stakes are not equal. For neither gold nor silver can be set against your person and the persons of your wife and children who are here; therefore we advise you not to put yourself or them in danger."

Then the king said, "Lords, I have heard your opinion and that of my people, and now I will tell you mine, which is this: If I leave the ship there are in her five hundred people and more who will land in this Isle of Cyprus, for fear of peril to their body—since there is none that does not love his life as much as I love mine— and these, peradventure, will never return to their own land. Therefore I like better to place my own person, and my wife, and my children in God's hands than do this harm to the many people who are here."

Their next adventure might have been more serious, at least for some of the crew. Sailing away in comparative safety in the damaged ship they came at length to the island of the sea called Pentelema, which was peopled by Saracens who were subjects of the King of Sicily and the King of Tunis.

"The queen begged the king to send thither three galleys to get fruit for the children; and the king consented, and ordered the masters of the galleys to go thither, and be ready to come back to him when his ship passed before the island. The galleys entered into a little port that was on the island; and it chanced that when the king's ship passed before the port, we got no tidings of the galleys.

"Then did the mariners begin to murmur among themselves.

"The king caused them to be summoned, and asked them what they thought of the matter. The mariners said it seemed to them that the Saracens had captured his people and his galleys.

"'But we advise and counsel you, sire, not to wait for them; for you are between the kingdom of Sicily and the kingdom of Tunis, which love you not at all. If, however, you suffer us to sail forward, we shall, during the night, have delivered you from peril, for we shall have passed through the strait.'

"'Truly,' said the king, 'I shall not listen to you, and leave my people in the hands of the Saracens without at least, doing all in my power to deliver them. I command you to turn your sails and we will fall upon them.'

"And when the queen heard this, she began to make great lamentation and said, 'Alas! this is all my doing!'

"While they were turning the sails of the king's ship and of the other ships, we saw the galleys coming from the island. When they came to the king, the king asked the mariners why they had tarried; and they replied that they could not help themselves, but that the fault lay with certain sons of burgesses of Paris, of whom there were six, who stayed eating the fruit of the gardens, wherefore they had been unable to get them off, nor could they leave them behind.

"Then the king commanded that the six burghers' sons should be put into the barge a-stern; at which they began to cry and to howl, saying, 'Sire, for God's sake, take for ransom all that we have, but do not put us there, where murderers and thieves are put; for we shall be shamed to all time.'

"The queen and all of us did what we could to move the king; but he would listen to none of us.

"So they were put into the barge, and remained there till we came to land; and they were there in such danger and distress that when the sea rose, the waves flew over their heads, and they had to sit down, lest the wind should carry them into the sea.

"And it served them right; for their gluttony caused us such mischief that we were delayed for eight good days, because the king had caused the ships to turn right about."

So at length Louis came to his own land of France; but his heart was full of longing for the "holy fields" of Palestine, and he was not content to live a life of luxury at the court while Jerusalem was yet in the hands of the infidel.

"After the king returned from overseas, he lived in such devotion that never did he wear fur of beaver or grey squirrel, nor scarlet, nor gilded stirrups and spurs. His clothing was of camlet and blue cloth, the fur on his coverlets and clothing was deer's hide, or the skin from the hare's legs, or lambskin. He was so sober in his eating that he never ordered special meats outside what his cook prepared; what was set before him that did he eat. He put water to his wine in a glass goblet, and according to the strength of the wine he added water thereto by measure; and would hold the goblet in his hand while they mixed water with his wine behind his table. He always caused food to be given to his poor, and after they had eaten, caused money to be given to them."

Thus, for the next fifteen years the king fulfilled the duties of his royal position in France; and all the while the voice of the East was calling, calling with insistent voice, as news of lost cities, quarrels between those who should have united themselves against the Saracens, and invasions of new and hostile races reached his ears.

CHAPTER XX

The Story of the Fall of Acre

"Because the chasuble is of red serge," said he, "that signifies that this Crusade shall be of little profit."

LE SIRE DE JOINVILLE: *Memoirs of St Louis.*

During the interval between the Eighth and Ninth Crusades, affairs in the Holy Land had gone from bad to worse.

The knights of the Hospital and Temple spent all their time in private quarrels and combats, and the merchants of Genoa and Pisa followed their evil example. The Moguls were continually harassing both Saracens and Christians, and when they were driven out by the combined forces of the two latter, the Sultan Bibars took the opportunity to seize the few towns that were left when the Crusade was over.

Nazareth was almost destroyed, Cæsarea, Joppa and Antioch fell, Acre was sorely threatened. In vain did Jerusalem call upon the Pope for help; his attention was fixed, not on Palestine but on Constantinople, where the Latin Empire had vanished, and a new Greek dynasty had been set up under Michael Palæologus. Absorbed in his desire to gain acknowledgment from this quarter, Clement IV. gave only half-hearted encouragement to a Ninth Crusade, yet he did succeed in stirring up enthusiasm in a somewhat unexpected quarter.

To England, still in the turmoil of the Baron's War, came the message of Clement reminding Henry III. of his old promise to take up the Cross; and the answer came, not from Henry, the inert and ineffective king, but from young prince Edward, his eldest son, moved perhaps rather by the expediency of employing his treasonable barons than by a keen desire for the freedom of Jerusalem.

One there was, however, who needed no urging, and had no base motives in his longing to start upon a Ninth Crusade. Saint Louis, as we have seen, had left his heart behind him in the Holy Land, and when he summoned all his barons to Paris in the Lent of 1267, it was not hard to guess the reason.

Among those who responded to the call went the Sire de Joinville, and, seeing how well he knew the mind of the king, it was no wonder that he should dream on the night of his arrival that he saw Louis on his knees, before an altar, whilst many prelates, duly vested, placed upon his shoulders a red chasuble of Rheims serge. Calling his chaplain, a very wise man, Joinville told him of the vision, and the priest at once said:

"Lord, you will see that the king will take the Cross to-morrow."

Joinville asked why he thought so; and he answered that it was because of the dream; for the chasuble of red serge signified the Cross; which was red with the blood that Christ shed from His side and His feet and His hands. "And because the chasuble is of Rheims serge," said he, "that signifies that the Crusade shall be of little profit, as you shall see if God gives you life," for Rheims serge was but poor and common material, and worth but very little.

So Joinville went to the king's chapel, and heard two knights talking there, one to the other. Then one said, "Never believe me if the king is not going to take the Cross here!"

And the other made answer, "If the king takes the Cross, this will be one of the most dolorous days that ever were in France. For if we do not take the Cross we shall lose the king's favour; and if we take the Cross we shall lose God's favour, because we shall not take it for His sake but for the sake of the king."

"So," adds Joinville, tersely, "it happens that on the following day the king took the Cross, and his three sons with him; and afterwards it befell that the Crusade was of little profit, according to the prophecy of my priest."

With this second expedition of Louis, Joinville himself had scant sympathy. He refused to join it on the ground that he owed a higher duty to his own poor and ruined people. And he held that those who advised the King to go "seeing how weak he was of body, for he could bear neither to drive nor to ride," were guilty of mortal sin.

"So great was his weakness that he suffered me to carry him in my arms from the mansion of the Count of Auxerre, where I took leave of him, to the abbey of the Franciscans. And yet, weak as he was, if he had remained in France, he might have lived longer and done much good and many good works."

However that might have been, Louis' work as a Crusader was well-nigh over. He left France accompanied by the Kings of Navarre and Aragon, and by many of his barons, and by sixty thousand of his men. Driven by a tempest to Sardinia, the leaders decided to turn aside to Tunis, whose king was suspected of being willing to become a Christian. Landing on the site of the ancient town of Carthage, they had but pitched their tents when a plague of sickness broke out in the camp, and the King and his son were the first to be struck down.

When he knew that his end drew very near, St Louis caused himself to be laid upon a bed of ashes, in token of his penitence, and all through that last night they heard him murmur at intervals, with longing in his voice, "Jerusalem! Jerusalem!"

But resignation to the Will of God was not difficult to a man whose character had been formed by a life of prayer and unselfish devotion.

"I will enter Thy house, O Lord, I will worship in Thy sanctuary," were the words of joy upon his lips, as he breathed his last.

"And it was at the same hour that the Son of God died upon the Cross for the world's salvation," says Joinville, who adds, moreover, the following touching tribute to the good king.

"A piteous thing and worthy of tears is the death of this saintly prince, who kept and guarded his realm so holily and loyally, and gave alms there so largely, and set therein so many fair foundations. And, like as the scribe who, writing his book, illuminates it with gold and azure, so did the said king illuminate his realm with the fair abbeys that he built, and the great number of alms-houses, and the houses for preachers and Franciscans, and other religious orders. And his bones were put in a casket and borne thence, and buried at St Denis, in France, where he had chosen his place of burial."

With St Louis died the deep religious side of the Crusades. Other kings had vague longings and desires, but none of them were driven to take part in the Holy War by the same fervent wish to lay down their lives for the Cause of God.

The work was now taken up by Edward, eldest son of the English King, Henry III. With him marched the great English nobles who had so lately been involved in the Barons' War; for Edward's main motive was to keep them employed and deprive them of opportunities for further rebellion.

Edward reached Tunis about seven weeks after the death of Louis, and found the camp in much disorder. The French barons were intent upon forcing the King of Tunis to pay tribute to the Sicilian sovereign, son of their late ruler, and were quite averse from proceeding at once on the Crusade. They all decided at length to go to Sicily for the winter, but the French Crusaders said openly that they wished the expedition deferred for at least four years. The death of the king and queen of Navarre and of the young queen of Louis' successor Philip the Bold, threw a gloom over their retreat, and before long all the French host returned to their native land.

Edward alone remained firm to his purpose, and in the following spring, with his little force of seven thousand men, he landed in Palestine. His first act was one of terrible revenge. Marching to Nazareth he took the town and put the Saracen inhabitants to the sword.

He then returned to Acre, only just in time to save the city from a Turkish raid; and there he seems to have had some curious intercourse with the Emir of Joppa, who pretended that he was anxious to become converted to Christianity.

But sickness fell upon Edward, and as he lay upon his bed, an assassin, sent as a bearer of letters from the Emir, gained admittance and struck the prince in the shoulder with a poisoned dagger.

Weak as he was, Edward had enough strength in reserve to grapple with the fellow, wrest the dagger from him and stab him to the heart. Doubtless the skilful nursing of his devoted wife, Eleanor, restored the prince to health, whether or no the story is true that she sucked the poison from the wound at the risk of her own life. The chronicles of the time give the credit to a clever young English doctor who cut away the poisoned flesh, but, however that may be, Edward had seen enough of the Holy Land to realise that his task was both dangerous and hopeless. When, therefore, letters from England urged his return on the score of his father's failing health, he hastened to make a ten years' truce with the Sultan, and to set out upon his homeward journey.

After his departure the old state of things was revived in the Holy Land. None knew who was in truth the rightful king, even in name, of the ill-fated kingdom of Jerusalem. The two great military orders of the Hospital and the Temple spent their time and energies in fighting with one another over their supposed rights; and the commercial rivalry of the Christian settlers from Genoa, Venice and Pisa, kept up a constant state of civil war which left them at the mercy of their enemies. In Acre, the one important town held by Christian rulers, so much fighting went on between the Christian inhabitants that much of the city had been quite destroyed.

Yet Acre was now the one hope, the one centre of Christianity in the Holy Land. To her walls had fled all those who had managed to escape when one town after another fell before the victorious march of the Sultan.

And so it came about that the city was filled with a mixture of nationalities, each of which claimed to be ruled by a separate authority. It was at one time governed by no less than seventeen rulers, "whence there sprang much confusion."

This wretched state of things did nothing more than stir up a feeling of mild uneasiness in Europe. Pope Gregory X., indeed, did his best to encourage a new Crusade, for he had been an eye-witness in Acre of the need of some active measure of reform. But he died before anything practical could be done. Some years later the Grand Master of the Templars made his way to the footstool of Pope Nicholas IV., and pleaded the cause of the hapless Christians.

The Pope, much moved, sent seventeen hundred mercenaries, or hired soldiers, at his own cost, to the relief of Acre; but these men, finding their wages were not paid, took to plundering the Saracen traders during a time of truce, and so earned for the Christians a worse reputation than ever.

These outrages, moreover, excited the indignation of the Egyptian Sultan, who prepared to attack Acre in the following spring, and meantime sent ambassadors to demand the surrender of the truce-breakers "under pain of open war." The Master of the Temple would have yielded to the justice of his demands, but the other political parties in the city were against any such idea, saying that it had always been the custom for the princes of the West to disregard any truce that might be of force in the East.

The views of the latter prevailed, and an embassy was sent to the Sultan, offering compensation, and assuring him that the offenders should be kept in prison till the truce had expired.

The Sultan Khalil listened in grim silence, and after a while replied with much dignity, "Your words are as the honey and sugar used to conceal the presence of a deadly poison. We have ourselves kept the truce with loyal intent, but such an offence cannot be suffered to pass unpunished. You may depart in full assurance that within the time appointed I will come against your city with a mighty host and destroy all, from the least to the greatest, by the sword."

Just before the return of the envoys with this threatening message, the spirits of the citizens had been much revived by the arrival in Palestine of Sir Otho de Grandison, the secretary and confidential friend of Edward I., with a small force and the information that Edward himself would shortly follow him.

The message of the envoys had filled the city with panic that was but slightly leavened with hope. They saw at length that their one chance lay in united action, and they determined to fight together for their city to the last. "And surely the princes oversea will send us timely help when they hear with what peril we are encompassed," was their cry.

Encouraged by their wish for unity the Patriarch sent them to their homes with the charge, "Be ye therefore constant, and ye shall behold the great help of the Lord come upon you."

So at length, when it was too late, all manner of energies were set to work. The city was refortified, a large store of arms was laid in, help was sent from Cyprus and the Islands of the Sea, until a force of nine hundred knights and eighteen thousand foot was within the walls. The care of the walls themselves was divided between Otho de Grandison, Henry, King of Cyprus, and the Master of the Teutonic Knights and the Masters of the Temple and the Hospital, with whom served the Masters of the Knights of the Sword and of the Knights of the Holy Ghost.

"These are the men," says one of the narratives of the survivors, "by whose prudence and counsel the city was to be governed. Had they been of one heart and mind, Heaven is our witness, Acre would still rejoice in the fulness of her strength." For alas, the old discord between the Templars and the Hospitallers had broken out afresh, and there was little hope of united action within the walls.

In the middle of March, the Saracens first appeared before Acre, "while making the earth to tremble at the march of their mailed men and to shake at the noise of their drums and cymbals; while the gilded shields of the soldiers flashed as the rays of the sun across the hills and their spearheads danced in the sunlight like stars in the midnight sky."

The din made before the walls was incessant. "They bellowed like bulls; they barked like dogs; they roared like lions; and ever, as is their wont, they drummed their huge tom-toms with their heavy-knotted sticks."

Then the war-engines were set up "which poured by day and by night a ceaseless hailstorm of stones upon the walls and city."

A partly successful sortie returned with some captives and the news that "the arrows were flying thicker than the flakes of snow in winter"; and on the Good Friday of the year 1291 Otho and the Templars planned a more united attack upon the Saracen camp. But this the Patriarch, acting on the advice of traitors, absolutely forbade, and so the last chance of saving the ill-fated city disappeared.

Many of the citizens and some of the fighting men now fled from Acre whenever they had the opportunity, but a considerable force yet remained, quite enough indeed to hold the city had they been content to work together. This, however, seemed impossible, and Khalil went boldly on to undermine the walls. The first direct assault was aimed at that section which was guarded by Henry of Cyprus, and only the nightfall prevented the Saracens from forcing an entrance. During the hours of darkness the King of Cyprus, with all his followers, crept to the harbour and secretly sailed away to his own island. And this he did, not so much in fear as in despair of ever accomplishing aught, when the petty quarrels and rivalries within the city left him without support.

This fatal policy of disunion was even more apparent during the last four days of that terrible siege. The Templars would not lift a hand to aid the Hospitallers; their bitter hostility made them more eager to fight each other than the infidel.

Meantime the Saracens had bridged the moat, broken through the outer walls, and driven the defenders to the inner part of the city. The captains, who were sitting in council, hastily donned their armour and rode forth into the midst of the panic-stricken crowd.

"Shame upon you!" they cried. "Fools! you are not hurt. To the battle with you, by the faith of Christ," and with Matthew de Clermont at their head, they charged upon the invaders and drove them out beyond the breach.

The Fall of Acre

261

The Fall of Acre

For three days this sort of thing continued, the Crusaders patching up the breach by night that had been broken in by day. But at daybreak of Friday, May 18, Khalil made his final assault. In the midst of the deafening noise made by his drummers mounted on three hundred camels, an attack was made upon all parts of the wall at once. Within a few hours the Masters of the Temple and the Hospital, rivals in life, were united in death. Overwhelmed by their loss, the Christians gave way, and though Otho de Grandison held out for awhile, it was soon clear that further resistance was impossible.

In the midst of the horror and confusion of the onrush of the Saracens through the doomed town, a terrific storm began to rage, while the sea rose to such a height that it became almost impossible to launch a boat or escape from the harbour.

The Patriarch had been carried aboard his own galley against his will, and in his wish to save as many of his people as possible, he allowed the vessel to be so overcrowded that she overturned, and all on board were lost. Many, however, did escape by water, and only a few, who had no desire save for righteousness, "remained behind to sell their lives dearly or to bargain with Saracen prisoners for their own lives."

Others held out in the Temple Tower, and when at length it fell, perished amid the ruins. Otho de Grandison was among those who managed to escape to Sidon, and afterwards to Cyprus.

So fell the last remnant of the Kingdom of Jerusalem, founded with such pride and devotion nearly two hundred years before.

CHAPTER XXI

The Story of the Fall of Constantinople

Men are we, and must grieve when even the shade
Of that which once was great has passed away.

WORDSWORTH: *On the Extinction of the Venetian Republic.*

No story of the Crusades can be complete without some account of the last scene in the drama that had been played for so many years between East and West, and which was ended for the time when Constantinople fell.

Since the year 1261, the Eastern Empire had passed out of the hands of Latin rulers, and once more owned an Emperor of Greek origin, Michael Palæologus by name. But this fact brought it no accession of vigour or strength. Worn out and impoverished, and lacking a great ruler who would have held the scattered threads of Empire in a firm grasp, the power of Constantinople was bound to lie at the mercy of a determined foe.

She had been already threatened, about the middle of the thirteenth century, by the dreaded Moguls, and only escaped because the latter first turned their attention to Russia. But the way to her final destruction was laid open by Michael the Emperor himself.

The borders of the Greek Empire in Asia had been guarded for many years past by the natives of Bithynia, the border state, who held their lands on condition that they kept the castles of the frontier in a state of defence.

Their task was no easy one, for the Seljukian Turks, who ruled over the neighbouring district of Iconium, were always on the watch to enlarge their boundaries; but these border militia were very faithful to their task, and had kept the invaders at bay.

Now Michael, formerly the Regent, had won the imperial throne by foul treachery towards the child Emperor, John Ducas, whose eyes he put out and whom he left to languish for thirty years in a wretched dungeon. Uneasy lies the usurper's head, and Michael could not rest until he had disarmed or got rid of all those who were suspected of loyalty towards the throne of Ducas.

Among these latter were the native "militia men" of Bithynia, whom Michael now proceeded to disband. The force substituted to defend the borderland was quite inadequate for the task; and the weakest spot on the frontier was thus left practically unguarded.

A few years earlier, a certain Othman, a Turk, had become the vassal of the Seljukian Sultan, and had been granted a district of the Phrygian highlands, on the very borders of the Greek Empire, on condition that he would take up arms against the Greeks.

Not many years passed before Othman, through the death of the last Sultan of the Seljuk line, had stepped into his place as an independent prince and the future founder of the Ottoman Empire. He outlived Michael Palæologus and his successor, and managed before his death to push the frontiers of the Turkish Empire forward to the Sea of Marmora.

His son Orkhan completed the conquest of Bithynia—a comparatively easy task now that the mistaken policy of the Greek Emperors had turned the troops of "hardy mountaineers into a trembling crowd of peasants without spirit or discipline."

By the year 1333, nothing remained of the Greek Empire in Asia but the town of Chalcedon and the strip of land that faced Constantinople across the straits.

The rule of the Ottoman Turks over their newly-conquered territory was firm and just enough, and was strengthened by material drawn from the ranks of the vanquished inhabitants. One of their demands was that a yearly tribute of young boys should be paid to them by the Christians. At first a terrible rumour spread that these children were killed and eaten by the infidels. But what really happened was that these boys were trained very carefully as soldiers, and became the "Janissaries," or "New Soldiers" of the

Ottoman army, against whom nothing could stand. They were forced, of course, to become followers of Islam, and they were appointed to all the highest offices of state. But their chief energy was reserved for the attacks made upon the land of their origin.

Gradually the Ottoman Turks crept nearer and nearer the heart of the Eastern Empire. A certain crafty Prime Minister of Constantinople, John Cantacugenus, in his determination to supplant his young sovereign, a child of nine, actually called in their aid and allowed them to over-run Thrace.

By the time that the usurper had won his way as joint ruler with his master, to the imperial throne, all that remained of the coveted empire was Constantinople, the towns of Adrianople and Thessalonica, and the Byzantine province in the Peloponnesus. His fatal alliance with the Turks had been cemented by a marriage between the Sultan Orkhan and his daughter Theodora; and when John Palæologus, the rightful sovereign, refused to submit to this arrangement of twin rulers, Cantacugenus at once called in his son-in-law to his help.

Once more the Ottomans swarmed into Thrace, and, though they found that Cantacugenus had been deposed and forced to become a monk, they were not disposed to retreat without some substantial indemnity. They seized upon and settled in a province of Thrace, and within two years had the whole district, together with the city of Adrianople, in their hands.

The next step was to the threshold of Constantinople itself, but for this the Turkish chieftain Murad was content to wait awhile. The capital was bound to fall in time, and he was first of all eager to make sure of his ground in Asia Minor.

During Murad's reign he extended his domain to the Balkans and up to the very walls of the imperial city; whilst the unhappy Emperor without an empire was thankful to escape for the present by acknowledging his supremacy, and even by taking up arms at his command against one of his own free towns.

For the next hundred and fifty years the Ottomans were only hindered from the invasion of Christendom by the determined action of the Servians and Hungarians. And meantime the chance of freeing the Greek Empire altogether from Ottoman rule had come and gone.

In 1402, when the Turkish Sultan Bajazet was pressing hard upon Constantinople, the great Tamerlane, chief of the Tartar hordes, who had already conquered Persia, Turkestan, Russia, and India, came down like a thunderbolt upon the ambitious plans of Bajazet. The latter defied the conqueror, saying, "Thy armies are innumerable? Be they so! But what are the arrows of the flying Tartar against the scimitars and battle-axes of my firm and invincible Janissaries?"

Alike in their religious faith and in their ambitions, these two men now became deadly rivals; but not even the "New Army" of the Ottoman could stand against the Tartar hordes.

One city after another fell and was sacked; Bajazet himself was taken, and imprisoned, according to one story, in an iron cage. Another and more modern version says that the great Tamerlane treated his captive with the utmost courtesy and consideration; and on the occasion of the victorious feast after the battle, placed a crown upon his head and a sceptre in his hand, promising that he should return to the throne of his fathers with greater glory than before. But Bajazet died before his generous conqueror could carry out his promises, and Tamerlane, taking his place, demanded tribute of his sons and of Manuel of Constantinople at the same time.

The two elder sons of Bajazet were now at variance over the poor remains of his empire. One of these bought the aid of Manuel by surrendering the coast of Thessaly and the seaports of the Black Sea, and the Emperor was able to keep these just so long as the war between the brothers continued to rage. Even after this had ended in the triumph over both of Mohammed, Bajazet's youngest son, Manuel could feel fairly safe, for of late years he had thrown in his lot with Mohammed and was allowed to hold his possessions in peace.

This period of civil war, was of course, the opportunity for the Greek ruler to have driven out the Ottomans from his former empire. But this opportunity was lost as so many others had been, and after Mohammed died in 1421, the empire was entirely surrendered to the Ottomans.

Mohammed's successor, Amurath, is thus described by one of his own historians. "He was a just and valiant prince, of a great soul, patient of labours, learned, merciful, religious, charitable; a lover and encourager of the studious, and of all who excelled in any art or science; a good Emperor and a great general.

"No man obtained more or greater victories than Amurath. Under his reign the soldier was ever victorious, the citizen rich and secure. If he subdued any country, his first care was to build mosques and caravanserais, hospitals and colleges. Every year he gave a thousand pieces of gold to the sons of the Prophet, and sent two thousands five hundred to the religious persons of Mecca, Medina and Jerusalem."

Like the Emperor Charles V, a century later, this "perfect prince" laid down the reins of empire at the very height of his glory and "retired to the society of saints and hermits," at Magnesia. Twice he was recalled to the field of action, first by an invasion of the Hungarians, the second time by the insurrection of the "haughty Janissaries "; and with these latter, now humbled and trembling at his very look, the great Amurath remained until his death.

Meantime the doomed city of Constantinople had been further weakened by internal strife. Hoping to get aid from the Pope, John Palæologus, the Emperor, had publicly conformed to the Roman Church, with many of his followers. But the bulk of the inhabitants of Constantinople utterly refused to throw over the ancient faith of the Greek Church, and preferred to disown their Emperor. As one of them ominously muttered: "Better the turban of the Turk in Constantinople than the Pope's tiara."

Disappointed of his hopes of any practical aid from Rome, John worked on in terrified silence while the brave King of Poland and Hungary tried in vain to drive back the triumphant Turks. He died only three years before the dreaded Amurath, and was succeeded by his brother Constantine, bearer of the honoured name of the founder of the city, but destined to be the last Christian ruler of the Eastern Empire.

Before very long, Constantine found himself face to face with the young Mohammed, the son of Amurath, who was already surnamed the Conqueror.

The all-absorbing desire of Mohammed was the possession of Constantinople, in order that it might be made the capital of his own Empire. Some pretence therefore must be found for a rupture with his meek vassal Constantine. At that time there dwelt within the city a certain Ottoman prince named Orkhan, much given to plots and ambitions, on whose account the Emperor was paid a considerable sum by Mohammed, on condition that he was kept from doing any harm. Very unwisely Constantine sent envoys to press for a larger payment, and even went so far as to try to blackmail the Sultan by hinting that Orkhan had the better right to the throne.

The reply of Mohammed was a prompt order to his engineers to construct a series of forts between Constantinople and the Black Sea, and thus to begin the siege by isolating the city from her port and food supplies. The actual excuse for warfare was provided in an attack made by some Greek soldiers on the Turks who were pulling down a beautiful old church in order to use its stones for their fort. The Greeks were promptly cut to pieces, and when Constantine dared to remonstrate, Mohammed at once declared war.

In vain did the despairing Emperor seek for help from the West. Even Genoa and Venice were blind to the approaching loss of all their Eastern trade, and Rome could do little to help. When the Emperor made a strong appeal to his own subjects to rally to the protection of their city, they listened in sullen silence to the words of one who had renounced the faith of his ancestors and conformed to the Church of Rome. There was never the smallest chance of holding out against the vigorous young Sultan and his picked troops.

In the spring of 1453 the actual siege began. Mohammed made use of that gunpowder which was to revolutionise all the ancient modes of warfare, and the old walls of Constantinople shuddered and fell before the shock.

The besieged had their guns too, but they did more harm than good, for the walls were too narrow to hold them and were so shaken by the concussion that these weapons had to be abandoned.

Yet for a time, owing largely to the courage and spirit of Constantine, the city not only held out, but succeeded in sending five vessels into the midst of the Turkish fleet, sinking and otherwise destroying all with which they came into contact. For allowing this to happen, the Turkish admiral, in spite of his plea of an injured eye as the cause of the mishap, was sentenced to receive a hundred strokes from a golden rod in the presence of the angry Sultan.

But this victory was quickly counterbalanced by Mohammed, who had some of his vessels brought overland across the neck that lies between the Bosphorus and the Golden Horn, thus shutting out the city from the sea on both sides. After a siege of forty days the end came on May 29, 1453. A special effort was urged by the Sultan in these words: "The city and the buildings are mine, but I resign to you the captives and the spoil, the treasures of gold and beauty; be rich and happy. Many are the provinces of my Empire; the intrepid soldier who first ascends the walls of Constantinople shall be rewarded with the government of the fairest and most wealthy; and my gratitude shall accumulate his honours and fortunes above the measure of his own hopes."

The answer came loud and strong from every part of the camp.

"Allah is great! There is no God but Allah, and Mohammed is His Prophet."

Within the city all was in gloom and despair. The Emperor was blamed for not surrendering earlier; many said that the "repose and security of Turkish servitude" were far preferable to this last stand for freedom.

The unfortunate Constantine listened in silence, and then went to the Cathedral of St Sophia, where he partook of his last Sacrament.

Rising from a brief and troubled rest at dawn, he mounted his horse to ride back to the breach in the falling walls. His few faithful friends and attendants pressed round the master who they knew was going to his death. Looking gravely down upon them, "he prayed one and all to pardon him for any offence that he might knowingly or unknowingly have committed against any man."

The crowd answered with cries and lamentations as he rode calmly to his fate. "The distress and fall of the last Constantine," says Gibbon, "are more glorious than the long prosperity of the Byzantine Cæsars."

Standing in the gap made in the wall by the Gate of St Romanus, the Emperor and his little band awaited the rush of the Janissaries. One by one his men fell behind him and at his side, until he alone remained.

One more attack was made, and this time the infidels swarmed right into the town, trampling the body of the Emperor underfoot. All that long and dreadful day the wail of the captives ascended to the heavens, and when a search was made among the dead, only the golden eagles on his shoes identified the crushed and disfigured form of him who once was Constantine, last of his race.

The last scene in the grim drama was played when the Sultan came to the Church of St Sophia, and, riding upon his magnificent war-horse, passed in through the eastern door and bade the Mullah pronounce the formula of the faith of Islam from the high pulpit.

"Allah is great! There is no God but Allah, and Mohammed is His Prophet!"

The words resounded through the aisles of the great eastern church, as they had echoed first in the desert of Arabia nearly nine hundred years before that day.

Through well-nigh nine centuries we have traced the growth of Islam, and the part played by the Holy War in hindering its progress to the West; and, having recorded this last and successful attempt of the Mohammedans at establishing themselves in

Europe, we will bring our story to an end with one last glance at the effect of this great movement upon Christendom.

CHAPTER XXII

The Effect of the Crusades

Oh, East is East, and West is West, and never the twain shall meet,
Till earth and sky stand presently at God's great Judgment Seat;
But there is neither East nor West, Border nor Breed nor Birth,
When two strong men stand face to face, though they come from the ends
of the earth.

RUDYARD KIPLING: Ballad of East and West.

The sacred fire of enthusiasm for the "Cause of God" still flickered faintly in Europe during the years that immediately preceded the fall of Constantinople. Our own Henry V., during his lifetime, sent out a knight of Burgundy, Gilbert de Lannoy, to see what chances there were of the success of a new Crusade; and Henry's dying words showed that he had not forgotten his design. "Good Lord, Thou knowest that mine intent had been, and yet is, if I may live, to rebuild the walls of Jerusalem."

But with the fall of Constantinople, all further hope of wresting the Holy Land from the infidel came to an end. Never again did a prince of the West set out to recover those "holy fields," and to this day they are ruled by the Sultan of Turkey.

It is said of Columbus that he had in mind the idea of stirring up an Eastern War in the "Cause of God" before there had dawned upon him the vision of that Western enterprise which was to open the gate to a new world. And that religious zeal did not die with the

Crusades is to be seen in the constant stream of pilgrims to the Holy Land which, for a hundred years, followed the final defeat of Christendom, and which, suspended though it was during the spiritual apathy of the eighteenth century, has continued down to the present day.

But the Age of Warfare was over when Constantinople fell, and with the dawn of that great awakening of thought and literature which we call the Renaissance, men turned away from bloodshed to the joys of discovery and enterprise in a new world.

A little later, when the Wars of the Reformation broke out, and Europe took up the sword anew, the whole spirit of the Western world had changed. The East had lost its glamour, and the antagonism between religious and political parties had waxed so hot in Christendom that the old feud between Christian and pagan was entirely laid aside.

Yet the Crusades, in spite of their apparent failure, had done a great work. First and foremost they had succeeded in deferring the rule of the Turk in Europe, and by the constant checks they offered to his progress, had prevented him from conquering anything but the merest fringe of the West. The advantage of this, apart from considerations of religion, will be seen at once if we compare the condition of the subjects of the Sultan with that of the more progressive of the Christian races of Europe.

But the benefits conferred upon Europe by the Crusades are by no means only of this negative character. The Saracen of the Middle Ages was a learned and cultured gentleman, skilled in medicine, in music, and in various other sciences, and, generally speaking, as much superior to the rough uneducated Crusader of the Western World as he was to the savage Ottoman Turk.

Foes though they were in name, there was always a certain amount of friendly intercourse between the Crusaders and the Saracens, and the former were bound to be affected in some degree by the civilisation of the latter. Sometimes a dark-faced "leech" would return in the train of a Crusading baron to Europe, and there would teach some of his mysteries of healing to the rough-and-ready doctors of the West.

To the Arabs we owe our "Arabic" system of numbers, used instead of the clumsy Roman figures, and the knowledge of the decimal notation, by which nearly every civilised country except our own reckons its money. From Architecture to Geography, all those branches of knowledge which distinguish the educated from the uneducated mind, may be traced back to the keen and subtle intelligence of the East.

Next perhaps in importance comes the opening up of the East to the West for purposes of Commerce. Many a knightly Crusader thought it no shame to carry on an extensive trade in the silks and spices of Palestine in order to fill his coffers upon his return and that he might be recompensed for the expenses of his undertaking. The constant crossing and recrossing of the Mediterranean soon set on foot a steady stream of commercial enterprise between the seaports of Italy and those of Syria, and the existence of a Latin Empire of Constantinople impelled Venice, the main cause of its establishment, to still closer communication with the East. To her, as "the Southern terminus of a great land trade-route," was carried the produce of England, Norway, Flanders, France and Germany as to a huge market, and she distributed it throughout the Eastern world, receiving in return the wealth of the latter to be carried back to Europe. It was only when the discovery of America opened up an entirely new field of enterprise that this great stream of commerce began to diminish.

Another effect of the Crusades was upon the great world of literature. Such a unique event as a Holy War was bound to inspire the writers of history even in the days when such writers were rarely to be found. William of Tyre was only one amongst several chroniclers of the First Crusade, and the story of the Crusades of later days have been vividly told by Richard of Devizes, Villehardouin and the Sire de Joinville, many of whose telling descriptions have been quoted in the pages of this book.

It was but natural that the gallant adventures of the Crusaders should form the theme of many of the epics and *chansons* of Chivalry. Charlemagne, Roland and Bevis of Hampton may never have seen the Holy Land, but they became the heroes of Crusading exploits nevertheless; while Richard Lion-Heart and Godfrey of

Boulogne, actual leaders in the Holy War, became the central figures of more or less impossible legendary adventures.

Through all this stream of literature ran that quickening, inspiring spirit of hope—perhaps the greatest gift of the Crusades to a world which, in the years between the Empire of Charlemagne and the Renaissance, might easily have fallen into a deadened condition of indifference and disruption.

This is scarcely the place to speak of the great unifying effect upon Europe, nor of the influence of the movement upon the feudal conditions of the time; but we have seen enough to know that the Western World was decidedly the better, spiritually, mentally and physically, for that gigantic failure which we know as the Crusades.

List of Books Consulted

The following books have been especially useful in the compilation of this little volume. My thanks are also due to Messrs Dent for permission to use some extracts from Sir Frank Marzials' charming translation of Villehardouin's Chronicle and that of the Sire de Joinville in their "Everyman" series.

Archer and Kingsford. *The Crusades; the Story of the Latin Kingdom of Jerusalem.*

Chronicles of the Crusaders by *Richard of Devizes, Geoffrey de Vinsauf and the Sire de Joinville.*

F. W. Cornish. *Chivalry.*

Sir G. W. Cox. *Crusades.*

W. E. Dutton. *History of the Crusades.*

J. F. Michaud. *History of the Crusades.*

H. Stebbing. *History of Chivalry and the Crusades.*

Gibbon's *Decline and Fall of the Roman Empire.*

CPSIA information can be obtained
at www.ICGtesting.com
Printed in the USA
BVHW040217261120
594270BV00019B/606

9 781977 832085